OVERCOMING SPIRITUAL SLUMP

Lenny Luchetti

OVERCOMING SPIRITUAL SLUMP

A Story of Acedia and
How God Can Get You Back in the Game

 Seedbed

Unless otherwise noted, Scripture quotations are taken from the Holy Bible, New
International Version®, NIV® Copyright © 1973, 1978, 1984, 2011 by Biblica, Inc.™
Used by permission of Zondervan. All rights reserved worldwide. www.zondervan.com
The "NIV" and "New International Version" are trademarks registered in the United
States Patent and Trademark Office by Biblica, Inc.™ All rights reserved worldwide.

Scripture quotations marked NASB are taken from the New American Standard
Bible®, Copyright © 1960, 1962, 1963, 1968, 1971, 1972, 1973, 1975, 1977,
1995 by The Lockman Foundation. Used by permission. www.Lockman.org.

Scripture quotations marked NLT are taken from the Holy Bible, New Living Translation,
copyright © 1996, 2004, 2015 by Tyndale House Foundation. Used by permission of
Tyndale House Publishers, Inc., Carol Stream, Illinois 60188. All rights reserved.

Printed in the United States of America

Cover design by Strange Last Name
Page design and layout by PerfecType, Nashville, Tennessee

Luchetti, Lenny
   Overcoming spiritual slump : a story of acedia and how God can get you back in the game /
Lenny Luchetti. – Franklin, Tennessee : Seedbed Publishing, ©2021.

   pages ; cm . + 1 videodisc

   ISBN 9781628249071 (paperback)
   ISBN 9781628249088 (Mobi)
   ISBN 9781628249095 (ePub)
   ISBN 9781628249101 (uPDF)
   OCLC 1252416940

   1. Acedia. 2. Spiritual life--Christianity. 3. David, King of Israel. I. Title.

BV4627.S65 L82 2021   241.3   2021939529

SEEDBED PUBLISHING
Franklin, Tennessee
seedbed.com

To Amy and Tim, braids in the rope
God used to pull me out of the slump.

CONTENTS

ACKNOWLEDGMENTS

My writing is done in physical isolation from other people, mostly because I'm all too easily distracted by anything that moves. Even Henry and Mabel, my dog and cat, steal my focus from the work of writing. No writer, though, truly writes alone. My life and this book are the result of the community in which I "live, move, and have my being" (see Acts 17:28). I am who I am because of God—the Father, Son, and Holy Spirit—and the church, my family, friends, and flock.

God "broke the bars of [my] yoke and enabled [me] to walk with [my head] held high" (Lev. 26:13b). That is, in short, the story of my life and the backdrop for *Overcoming Spiritual Slump.* To tell you the truth, a few of the personal details I recount in the following pages elicit some shame in me. Then I remember the grace of God, "my glory, the

One who lifts my head high" (Ps. 3:3b). I believe God has given me the grace to write this book with the brutal, even humiliating, honesty necessary to help disciples who feel stuck in stagnancy.

The church has had a major role in this book's development. While teaching seminary classes; preaching at camps, colleges, and congregations; and sipping coffee with my family and friends I have beta tested the observations, ideas, and hopes sprinkled throughout the following pages. The frequent response to the beta test was: "So many of us struggle with the spiritual slump and we need a hopeful process for getting unstuck." Their affirmation gave me the courageous compassion to write what follows.

The Seedbed Publishing team, led by Andy Miller, provided the nudge I needed to cross the finish line. Their passion for loving Christ and resourcing the church is contagious.

INTRODUCTION

I was a secret slumper. Most people knew me as a seminary professor, a pastor to pastors, and a published author in demand as a speaker for clergy and church events. But deep down in my soul, where only God could see, I was struggling with spiritual stagnation for several years. Praying, reading the Bible, and communing with other Christians seemed more appalling than appealing to me, more like a root canal or colonoscopy than a delight. I was in big trouble and didn't care. What's worse, I didn't care that I didn't care. For the first time in my life I experienced what early Christians called "acedia." Acedia is spiritual apathy that causes one to slowly drift from the divine. I was stuck smack-dab in the middle of a spiritual midlife crisis.

Acedia, a lack of passion for God, was a new experience for me. Ever since entering into a friendship with God

1

through Christ at age eighteen, my heart beat strong for him. Here's the backstory. Previous to my conversion, I was a mess; so low I could wear a top hat and walk under a snake. My parents, whom I adored, were battling an addiction to heroin. Heroin was winning. I needed an escape from the fear and shame. Cheap beer with a chaser of pot became my bosom buddies. Quickly, they became dominating bullies who led me to places I didn't really want to go.

By the time I was sixteen I was an alcoholic, getting drunk several times each week. In the fall of my junior year of high school, I concluded it was nearly impossible to be a student and a drunk. One of them had to go, high school or the high life. I decided to abstain from school. Now I could get drunk without having to wake up hungover for school in the morning. Yippee! I had no money but was living with my grandmother, who always seemed to forget how much was really in her purse. Lucky me.

The urban, vice-infested streets of Philadelphia were the stage for my five-alarm wake-up call. I was drunk, high, and bored. I started a fight with a guy in his twenties for no other reason but to entertain me and my crew of friends, who were almost as intoxicated as I was, but not quite. I walked up to the guy, my beer muscles growing with every step, and landed a right hook to his head. Seeing I had a sizable posse, he ran. I chased him. When he saw I was alone, he turned to me and put up his hands, Ali-style. I ran toward him with another right hook, so drunk I failed to see the knife in his left hand. But I felt it. The blade traveled four inches into my right side, puncturing my lung. I almost died, but was internally dead already.

The several days I spent in the hospital attached to a chest tube gave me time to reflect on my dismal life. I internally and intuitively admitted the first two steps of AA: "I'm in trouble and I need help." Not long after my four-day vacation at the Methodist Hospital in South Philly, I went on another vacation. Since high school wasn't getting in my way, I suppose I had the time to see the world. I went to an all-inclusive resort in Syracuse, New York, called Teen Challenge, a Christ-centered drug and alcohol rehabilitation center. The lodging and food weren't five-star, not even close, but the excursions into Christ were transformational. Along with my parents who were in recovery, I entered into a life-saving, dignity-bestowing, and hope-inducing relationship with Jesus Christ. Friends and family members who knew me best back then acknowledged the miracle of me not only being physically, but fully, alive.

I thrived in loving and being loved by Christ for decades. I could exclaim with King David, featured prominently in the following pages, that God "lifted me out of the slimy pit, out of the mud and mire; he set my feet on a rock and gave me a firm place to stand" (Ps. 40:2). His love lifted me and I never looked back. I remember judging other Christians who seemed stale and lukewarm. I was so grateful for grace, like the younger son in the parable of the prodigal in Luke 15. Many longtime churchgoers seemed like the older son in the parable: dutiful but distant. *Where is the joy of their salvation?* I judgmentally pondered.

Perhaps because of my abysmal past, passionate fervor for God was as effortless as breathing. That is, until decades later, when I found myself stuck neck-deep in the mud and mire of a spiritual slump that was kicking the you-know-what out of me. I was in my early forties, experiencing symptoms of a midlife crisis. Only I wasn't fantasizing about a Corvette or a hottie half my age.

My spiritual midlife crisis was more about what I didn't want than what I wanted. I lost my appetite for Scripture. I didn't want to pray. One of the only prayers I did pray was: "God, make me want to want you more." I didn't want to be with people, especially happy-go-lucky types oozing with the joy of the Lord. I didn't want to counsel, preach, teach, or write. All I wanted to do on most days was stay in bed and watch reruns of *Law and Order*, *Criminal Minds*, and, when things were really bad, PBS's *Downton Abbey*. But I had too much to do and too much pride not to do it.

Oh, I almost forgot. A desire for my old pal alcohol was welling up in me during those intense days of acedia. It had been nearly twenty years since we were besties. I'm ashamed to admit I spent more time fantasizing about extra hoppy craft beer burning its way down my throat into my belly than I savored the flavor of God's amazing grace.

The hardest part of being in a spiritual slump is the lonely isolation. *Who can handle my junk? Who can I let into my struggle?* I was more concerned about losing my job as a seminary professor and my respect as a Christian leader than I was about losing my soul. For far too long I kept my spiritual midlife crisis bottled up like a genie. The secret slump starved my soul.

Pride and fear kept me from sharing my story publicly (until now). God persisted and I finally relented. Someone like me, a pastor and professor to pastors, is not supposed to get stuck in a spiritual slump. But I did, and for years. It was humiliating until I discovered I'm not alone. Some of the most beautiful people I know, who are vibrant and fully alive, have suffered through the spiritual slump. This book, then, depicts not just my story but the story of numerous disciples who have battled the slump of acedia. Perhaps it will reflect your story, too, in a way that annihilates loneliness and induces hope.

Every single person, I'm convinced, will experience staleness or stagnation at some point. You are likely heading into, going through, or coming out of a spiritual slump. We will likely endure several seasons of aridity in our lifetimes. These are intense seasons when your appetite to be with God through prayer and Scripture, and to live for God through trust and obedience, diminish like air slowly leaking from a tire. Danger abounds. You are vulnerable to old temptations you thought were in the rearview mirror and new ones that pop up like moles you're not fast enough to whack!

You are not alone, even though few have the language or the courage to talk about their struggle. You are not stuck, even though you feel neck-deep in mud. There is a way out of the staleness, the stagnancy, the slump. The story of how God brought me out of the slump will be continued in the conclusion. For now, know that God has given us tools for overcoming the slump that can make our lives more vibrant and meaningful than before we even started to slump. What I'm asserting is that a spiritual slump can deepen rather than destroy us, if we can grab onto the rope of God's grace and hold on for dear life. It has been said, "The same sun that melts the wax also hardens the clay." Every problem is potential for growth. How we navigate the slump will determine the sort of person we become and the kind of life we live.

The Bible is replete with people who endured the spiritual slump like the one you or someone you love might be stuck in right now. Moses slumped into murderous anger. Abraham slumped into manipulative lying. Peter slumped into fearful denial. And these are the so-called heroes of the biblical story! They slid down the slippery slope of disappointment with and distance from God that made them vulnerable. But, and this is a really big "but," they overcame the spiritual slump by grasping God's grace at their lowest points. So did I. So can you!

No one epitomizes how to get into, go through, and come out of the spiritual slump quite like King David. Let's explore the spiritual journey of this shepherd boy turned warrior king as he moves from degeneration to disruption to detestation to disclosure to decision and, by God's grace, overcomes the spiritual slump.

Reflection

- What do you think causes acedia, the apathy of the spiritual slump?
- Have you ever endured a spiritual slump? What was that experience like? Did it make you better or bitter?
- Do you know of someone who went through a spiritual slump and came out on the other side a deeper, more vibrant disciple?
- Do you agree that most, if not all, Christians will experience a spiritual slump at some point in their journey? Why or why not?

Prayer

Lord, I'm reading this book to grab hold of your grip of grace. Pull me out of the slump and place my feet on solid rock. Do for me what I cannot do for myself. Replace my staleness and stagnancy with fervent love. "Restore to me the joy of your salvation" (Ps. 51:12a). Amen.

| 1 |

Degeneration

Degeneration is a gradual descent into spiritual boredom, complacency, and, ultimately, compromise.) The degenerating disciple experiences distance from God that often fosters disobedience and, in time, despondence. A person in this predicament is tempted to cease seeking and obeying God. There is a general lack of care—a spiritual apathy—that leads smack-dab into a spiritual slump. The newly crowned King David experienced devastating degeneration.

The Baseball Slump

If you're a baseball fan the terms *streak* and *slump* are familiar to you. A streak is when a player gets a hit to get on base game after game. The record for the hitting streak is held by Joe DiMaggio, who, in 1941 with the New York Yankees, got a hit to get on base in fifty-six consecutive games. A streak is a good thing for a ball player. A slump is not. When a player fails to get a hit to get on base game after game, it's called a slump. The record for the longest slump in major league baseball history is held by Chris Davis, who, in 2019 with the Baltimore Orioles, went 0 for 54. He came up to bat fifty-four times and didn't get on base once! That's one sorry slump!

Lots of players go from streak to slump in their career. They start off on a hot streak and then fizzle into a slump. Some slumping players end up back in the minor leagues or out of the game of baseball entirely. Streak. Slump. Retire. Here are a couple of notable examples.

Brian Doyle was great. He was brought up to the major league at age twenty-three because of a late-season injury to the great Willie Randolph in 1978. Doyle had a batting average of .438, which is outstanding, and helped the Yankees win the World Series in his first season. After that, his career batting average was a horrific .161 (in just 110 regular-season games in the pros). Streak then slump then out of the game!

Joe Charboneau is another notable. He looked like the savior of the Cleveland Indians franchise. They called him "Super Joe." He hit twenty-three home runs and batted .289 in 1980, his rookie season. He won the American League Rookie of the Year Award. And then he wasn't that anymore. The eccentric Charboneau, known for opening beer bottles with his eye socket and doing his own dental work, hit just six more home runs in his career. He was demoted to the minor leagues in 1981. In 1984, just a few years after his incredible rookie season, Super Joe was completely out of pro baseball. Streak then slump then out of the game!

The Spiritual Slump

This happens all the time in baseball. Players go from a hitting streak to a hitting slump. Some never recover. They get demoted to the minors or quit playing. It happens in the church too. The new Christian starts off with a bang, a streak, and then flattens out or falls out of the game. Do you know disciples like this? One minute they're passionately in love with Christ and the next the love tapers off. Their best days in Christ are behind them, it seems, not before them. They spend the rest of their life trying to get back to the good ole days of their early walk with Christ, their rookie season spiritual streak. They go to camps and retreats, hoping to get back on a spiritual hitting streak. Know someone like this? Maybe you are that someone.

I know a guy who went from streak to slump. Early on, he thrived in his relationship with God. He came out of the box batting .1000. He was, as they say, on fire. He trusted God so much he was crazy enough (I mean, faithful enough) to do anything God called him to do regardless of the risk and sacrifice involved. He possessed a rare, zealous love for God. He enjoyed victory after victory. Spiritually speaking, he was on a hot streak.

But something happened. He became bored and complacent. His compromises were small at first. He shirked his responsibilities at work. Being a high-level executive, he could use his position to get away with pretty much anything. And he did. He neglected his marriage and slipped into coexistence with his spouse. He didn't worship and pray as often or with the passion of his hitting-streak days. The increasing distance from the Lord allowed him the space to compromise in bigger ways. Distance led to disobedience, and he did unthinkable things he never imagined doing. He had an affair with a married woman. She got pregnant with his child. In order to cover up his infidelity, he used his power to get her husband killed. Streak to slump.

Perhaps by now you recognize this severe slumper. He is one of the so-called heroes of the biblical story. His name is David. He experienced what every slumping Christian does—degeneration. (Degeneration is a change to a lower state or level; a gradual sinking and wasting away of mind, body, or spirit; a descent to a state of low moral standards and behavior.] How did a spiritual slugger like David degenerate into a spiritual slump?

David's Streak to Slump

(David was the youngest son of Jesse, a runt, a shepherd boy, a nobody really.) Apparently, David was so lacking in potential that Jesse didn't even present him to Samuel, who was to anoint one of Jesse's sons to be the next king of Israel. David's own dad didn't think David had the goods to be king. Few things in life hurt more than having a dad who doesn't see your potential, who doesn't think much of you.

However, David's divine dad highly valued him. God gave David one miraculous victory after another, starting with Goliath and ending with the Ammonites and Arameans. David was divinely promoted from shepherd to king. Everything he did prospered. Everything! This repeated phrase sums up the early days: "the Lord gave David victory wherever he went" (2 Sam. 8:14; 1 Chron. 18:13). David was not a self-made but a God-made man. God picked up this shepherd and turned him into a king. God was determined to bless David.

God favored David, and David adored God. First Samuel 17 highlights David's youthful zeal. Faced with Goliath-sized challenges, David saw nothing but God. He said to the Philistine giant, "You come against me with sword and spear and javelin, but I come against you in the name of the LORD Almighty . . . whom you have defied. . . . This day the LORD will deliver you into my hands" (vv. 45–46a). David had a one-track mind. He saw past the Goliath-sized problems to the God-sized possibilities.) David kept his eyes on the ball, on God, not Goliath. A slumping player once asked the comedic Yogi Berra for hitting advice. Berra said; "If you can see it, hit it." Thanks, Captain Obvious! David saw God and hit the ball out of the park. He was on a spiritual hitting streak. Red hot!

(The problems started when David became king at age thirty. On the mountaintop of success, complacency surfaced. David found himself stuck in a spiritual midlife crisis, a slump. The ardent love for God that marked his youth diminished. In the slump, David discovered that the biggest Goliath he had to overcome was not Goliath, not the Philistines, not King Saul, and not the Ammonites. The biggest Goliath David had to conquer was David; David nearly destroyed David.)

Slipping into a Slump

Every one of us likely has at least one terrible, horrible, no good, very bad chapter of regret, failure, or humiliation that we'd like to rip out of the story of our lives. I do. For David, the literal chapter is 2 Samuel 11. "At the time when kings go off to war" (v. 1), King David stayed within the palace walls of safe status quo. He was bored in his boxers, channel surfing between his favorite sitcoms. He dragged himself off the sofa and onto the palace rooftop looking for something—anything—to make him feel something— anything—again. He noticed a beautiful woman taking a bubble bath, who was rightly named Bathsheba. One thing led to another, and David invited her to the palace. He slept with her, even though he knew she was married to Uriah, a soldier out fighting David's battle. Bathsheba became pregnant with David's baby. In order to keep the adulterous pregnancy a secret, David had Uriah killed on the battlefield.

Talk about slumping degeneration! Boredom to lust to adultery to murder. Sports journalists love to write catchy headlines for slumping players: "Jeter's Slump Killing Yankees" or "Pujols' Slump the Most Expensive in MLB History." At the end of this terrible chapter in David's story, here is the horrific headline hanging over his head: "The thing David had done displeased the LORD" (v. 27b).

What happened to David between the streak and the slump? What happened between "the LORD gave David victory wherever he went" (2 Sam. 8:14) and "the thing David had done displeased the LORD" (2 Sam. 11:27b)? He backslid. He stopped taking faith-filled risks. He played life safe. David's military campaigns were sort of vocational for him. That's how he served God. Military conquest was David's "spiritual act of worship," how he rolled with God. Some people pray and preach, but David fought. The fact that he stayed in the Jerusalem palace "at the time when kings go off to war" reveals that midlife boredom was getting the best of him.

How does someone like David, full of fervent love for God, seemingly all of a sudden commit adultery and then murder to cover his tracks? Well, I don't think it happened all of a sudden. There's evidence that David's spiritual slump started long before the rooftop lust of 2 Samuel 11. Five times in David's story we encounter the phrase, "David inquired of the LORD" (1 Sam. 23:2, 4; 30:8; 2 Sam. 2:1; 21:1). David habitually sought the will of God. David lived like he was deeply dependent on God's guidance. But in between 2 Samuel 6, the chapter after David is crowned king, and 2 Samuel 11, when David commits adultery and murder, we only encounter the phrase once (see 2 Samuel 2:1). Once David became king, it seems he outgrew his need for God.

Like a baseball player who stops caring, David neglected the disciplines that cultivated his game. He was like the slumping ball player who stops taking batting practice, exercising, and working with his hitting coach. At the peak of his game, when there was more on the line than ever, David let his game go. Now the former spiritual slugger can't hit the broad side of a barn. He struck out with the bases loaded in the bottom of the ninth inning down by one run. David stopped doing the one thing that got him on a spiritual streak—inquiring of the Lord. (David's degeneration was not initiated by lust, adultery, or murder, but neglect.)

You stop inquiring when you stop caring. This is true of any relationship, especially marriage. Couples discover that a lack of inquiry leads to a lack of intimacy. I'm not talking about shallow inquiries like: "Do these pants make me look frumpy?" or "Does my breath stink?" Couples that thrive engage in substantive inquiries like: "How can I love you better?" and "What are worthy goals for our next ten years together?"

David stopped inquiring of the Lord and discovered the hard way that a lack of inquiry leads to a lack of intimacy. (Distance from God allowed David the space to be disobedient in ways he likely never imagined possible. When we're distant from God, he seems smaller than the Goliaths all around us.) How does a pastor who has been fruitful for thirty years of ministry find himself slumping into an affair with his secretary? How does a woman known for honesty and integrity end up slumping into a double life of pain-pill popping? How does a once faithful teenager slump into an addiction to porn? A lack of inquiry leads to a lack of intimacy. Distance creates space for disobedience.

Despondence

When we keep striking out spiritually due to our disobedience, we eventually experience despondence. If you read *The Pilgrim's Progress*, John Bunyan's classic, you might recall the slough of despondency. Despondence can be described with some other nasty "D" words like depression, despair, discouragement, and dejection. It is a loss of hope that things can change. In my research on the baseball slump, I discovered that what often keeps a player stuck is not his mechanics but his despondence, the loss of hope that he can improve his hitting. The same thing is true regarding the spiritual slump. What perpetuates the slump is the belief that we can't overcome the slump, that we are stuck, that we will never improve our discipleship swing.

Christians who are despondent about overcoming the spiritual slump often embrace a warped view of grace that leads to excusing instead of eradicating sin. We start comparing ourselves favorably to people whose slump seems more despicable than our own. Pride becomes a deadly poison that leads deeper into spiritual degeneration.

David went from streak to slump. Distance led to disobedience to despondence to degeneration. Did David settle for the spiritual slump? Did he conquer it? Or did he end up like one of those washed-up ball players who start strong but quickly fade into the minor leagues or out of the game altogether?

Minor League Christianity

Too many Christians confess that, while they still love Jesus, their love has plateaued or declined. They are in a relationship that feels more like coexistence than intimacy. They share the chores and pay the bills with Jesus. There are quick conversations in passing but no depth of discussion. Inquiring of the Lord happens infrequently at best, but rarely at the depth necessary for holy intimacy.

More Christians than you might imagine confess that they are not where they could be or used to be in Christ. They are no longer in Egypt, the land of slavery, but not yet in Canaan, the land of promise. They are in the wilderness of the spiritual slump, no longer a slave but not fully free. As a pastor and professor to pastors, I've had countless conversations with disciples who are striking out in the wilderness.

Why do so many Christians feel stuck in minor league living, existing off the glory days of the past? Why are so many of us tempted to slip back into some destructive Little League hitting habits? Why does it seem so hard to keep Christ as the burning passion of our lives, like he was when he first raised us from death to life? Why do other competitors—relationships, hobbies, possessions, physique, career, and ministry, to name a few—become more central to our lives than the Christ who saved us? Why do so many of us, like David, fall out of love with and stop inquiring of God? When we become more enamored with someone or something other than God, we step onto the slippery slope of the spiritual slump.

It can happen to the best of us. When I was battling through my slump several years ago, I initiated a breakfast with one of my spiritual heroes. He's in his seventies and is fragrant with the aroma of Christ. This friend has mentored many Christians throughout his life. He is vibrant and wise. When I confessed, with some embarrassment, that I was in a spiritual slump, he shocked me with the same confession. He lamented, "I feel like I've plateaued. I find myself not wanting to pray or read Scripture." I was stunned, yet comforted that I wasn't alone in my struggle.

The more I share my journey of battling the spiritual slump, the more I realize how common the struggle is for many people. There are numerous Davids in the church who have stopped going off to war. They are, spiritually speaking, bored in their boxers or bathrobe. Lethargy, apathy, and acedia have infiltrated their faith. If one hundred Christians were randomly surveyed and asked to rate their level of joyful intimacy with God on a scale from 1 to 10, I suspect that more than 50 percent would offer a 4–6 rating or lower. That's a slump. God didn't create us for mediocrity, but for intimacy.

When Christians stay in the slump for a long time they will revert back to old, unhelpful hitting habits. Jake was a gifted musician heading into ministry to proclaim Christ. Then, he was in and out of jail for violence and stealing. Slump! Michelle clung to Christ through her difficult divorce and was spiritually thriving. Then, she became hypercritical of everyone and everything in the church. Slump! Steve was on fire for God and getting his life on track through our church's addiction recovery ministry. Then, he overdosed on pills. Slump! When someone once in love with God goes off the spiritual deep end, like David who covered up adultery with murder, a lengthy slump is usually the culprit.

Slump Statistics and Symptoms

Stats don't lie. Serious ball players will keep a close eye on their statistics. They will find out how many times they struck out in the last fifty at bats. They know their batting average, on-base percentage, and slugging percentage. A ball player knows that if he is striking out five of every ten times at bat, something is wrong. He is aware of his rate at hitting the fastball, curveball, and slider. If he did not get on base in eight of the last ten times at bat, he is on the verge of a slump and knows it. The first step in overcoming the slump is to recognize that you're in one. To do that, you have to scan the stats.

The Christian has statistics too. An "at bat" for the Christian is every opportunity we have to love God or not love God in word, thought, or deed. It would be easy to overlook the slump. Courage is required to probe the stats and do some life inventory. Let's give it a go.

When someone hurt us and we were up to bat with a chance to forgive or retaliate, did we get a hit or strike out? When we heard that racist joke at the workplace, did we confront the stereotype or laugh, crush the ball or strike out, love God or not love God? When we were home alone with the computer or phone, tempted to click or swipe on what we know to avoid, did we decide to love God or not love God? Did we get a hit or strike out? When we had a chance to give our time to serve the purposes of God, did we give or withhold, love God or not, get a hit or strike out? When we were up at the plate with a chance to speak a word that builds someone up or breaks someone down, did we love God or not, get a hit or strike out? The kind of ball player we become on the playing field of life is determined by the accumulation of choices we make to love God or not love God in word, thought, and deed.

The scariest thing about the spiritual slump is not recognizing when you're in one. The thoughts in my head, the words in my mouth, and the actions of my hands provide the data for the slump scan. The goal of the scan is not guilty condemnation but gracious liberation. Too many Christians who have been raised with Christ are now dead people walking, zombies stuck in a slump. And we will stay zombie-like unless we have the capacity to see and admit the slump.

Still not sure you're going through a spiritual slump? Here are some slump symptoms. If you are reading the Bible less or not at all because you deep-down doubt that you will receive a word from the Lord from the Word of the Lord, you may be in a spiritual slump. If you stop praying with fervor because you are convinced God is too disappointed with you or you are too disappointed with him, you may be in a spiritual slump. If you quit serving people because you don't feel appreciated or affirmed, you may be in a spiritual slump. If fellowship with other Christians seems more painful than productive, like a trip to Walmart on the eve of a major holiday, you may be in a spiritual slump. If you look for diversions to keep you from seeing the slump, such as food, social media, and reruns of *Friends*, *The Office*, or *Duck Dynasty*, you may be in a spiritual slump. If you think about God less and fantasize about sin more, you may be in a spiritual slump. If you stop believing, trying, and hoping, you may be in a spiritual slump.

God's Grace: Our Hope

Hall of Famer Frank Robinson had one of the greatest rookie seasons in baseball history. In his second season, however, he went 0 for 20 at bats. Thirty-five years later Robinson acknowledged, "I didn't think I was ever going to get another hit." Robinson overcame the slump to become one of the greatest baseball players ever. The slump was not merely an obstacle, but an opportunity that propelled him to a higher level of play.

Maybe you feel like you will never hit the ball again. Maybe you feel like your best days in Christ are behind, not before, you. Maybe you feel better suited for minor league Christianity or want to retire from discipleship completely. I get it. But realize that working through a slump can actually make you a better disciple than you were before the slump. There is a bright shining light of joy at the end of the journey through the tunnel.

Over time, the slump can destroy or deepen a person. Some disciples throw their hands up and accept the slump.

Others quit and hang up their spiritual cleats. Then there are the brave ones who overcome the slump and come out of it every inch a passionate Christ-follower, better than ever. Your willingness to read this book and work through the slump puts you on the path to being one of the overcomers.

What happened to David? The bad news is he hit rock-bottom. The good news is God found him there. Countless kings after David never overcame their spiritual slump. But David followed God through a process that brought him out of the slump and put him back on a streak again. We will probe that transformational process as we journey through the following pages. For now, know that God will not give up on you even if you have given up on yourself. When you find yourself stuck in a slump, God will find you there. It's called grace. Disruptive grace is the focus of the next chapter.

Reflection

- On a scale from 1 to 10, how would rate your current level of joyful intimacy with Christ?
- Are you currently in a spiritual slump? Have you ever been in a spiritual slump? Reflect on the causes and consequences of your slump.
- What symptoms of the spiritual slump have you experienced?

- Do you inquire of the Lord on a consistent basis? If so, what's the evidence? If not, why not?
- Do you know someone who has overcome the spiritual slump? What practices or resources did they engage to grab God's grace?

Prayer

God, "Hound of Heaven,"[1] sniff out those of us who are in a slump and despondent because of it. Rescue those who are on the verge of giving up hope that they will ever hit the ball again. Give us the capacity to assess whether or not we're in a slump and the courage to admit it to ourselves. God of grace, help us out of the slump and get us back on a streak that glorifies you and inspires people. We pray in the name of the Christ who came to save slumping sinners, amen.

| 2 |

Disruption

Disruption is not a nuisance but a grace when God initiates it. Disciples who are stuck in a spiritual slump of degeneration cannot save themselves no matter how hard they try. They need a force outside of them, more powerful than them, to disrupt their degeneration. Only a rope of grace will save the stuck. The way God lovingly disrupted David's degeneration is hope-inducing for slumping disciples.

Quiet Desperation

King David messed up royally. He was stuck with Krazy Glue to spiritual malaise. Whether or not he knew it, he was desperate. The spiritual slugger seemed ready to retire and hang up his cleats.

Henry David Thoreau is frequently quoted as saying, "The mass of men lead lives of quiet desperation." Slumping Christians sense this quiet desperation deep in their soul. They feel their best discipleship days are in the past with the Carmen and Sandi Patty cassettes, DC Talk and Petra CDs, or Relient K, Lecrae, and Switchfoot MP3s. They are not necessarily reverting back to Little League discipleship, but they are not loving God at a major league level either. They are meandering in minor league. They are still in Christ and haven't lost their salvation, but something's off. Their spiritual lives are in limbo, a sort of purgatory between the hell of their past and the heaven of their future.

I know from pastoral experience that even good, church-going people can get stuck in a spiritual slump. Compromise here, neglect there, and—voilà—slump! Some still have an ounce of hope that they will get back on a streak again. Others conclude with quiet desperation that they will never become the slugger they envisioned. They imagine a horrific headline hanging over their head like: "the thing David had done displeased the LORD" (2 Sam. 11:27b).

Maybe your self-designated horrific headline is: "Just an Average Christian Stuck in a Perpetual Slump" or "Destined for Spiritual Mediocrity." Part of the battle in overcoming the spiritual slump is recognizing and remediating warped self-perceptions.

Slump Starters

There are several slump starters—past regret, present sin, and future fear. Each one has the power to throw us into acedia. All of them together can suffocate the soul.

Past regret does present damage. All of us likely have something in our past that nags at us. Maybe it was an embarrassing moment that humiliated you. Maybe it was a bad decision that hurt you or a loved one. You neglected an important relationship you can't repair. You said destructive words you can't take back. You lied and forfeited your integrity. You had an abortion. You committed adultery. You didn't tell a friend about Christ before she died. You got divorced. You became addicted. You can't undo what you did. You can't go back in time and make things right. You can't get your relationship back, your job back, your dignity back, your reputation back, or your opportunity back. Your absolute inability to undo the past leaves you in a spiritual slump of regret. The past can be a prison that prohibits present progress.

Sarah was an outstanding wife and mom to her two kids. When she hit midlife she had, in her words, "a nervous breakdown." She started abusing drugs, which eventually abused her. She would shoplift and steal money from her family to get high. This incredible mom was undone by drugs right before the eyes of her kids. Shame hung around her neck like a ball and chain.

Miraculously, she went into rehab, found Christ, and got clean. But deep inside she carried the shame of past regrets. There was no way to undo the damage to her kids, no way to get those years back when she was strung out. While she loved God, she saw herself as a mediocre disciple at best. In her mind, she was destined for minor league Christian living because of her regretful past. She was engaged in self-flagellation because of her past.

Present sin can cause a spiritual slump. Most sins these days can be traced back to the tongue and technology, or "TNT." They are dynamite, the bad kind. ("The tongue also is a fire, a world of evil among the parts of the body" (James 3:6a).) Now the fiery tongue has a large platform, thanks to technological advances. As a society we have become ruthlessly loose with the tongue via social media. Envious put-downs, harsh one-sided criticism, boasting, gossiping, and myopic meanness are easy to locate on social media. The subtle sins of social media can consume a person over time and thrust them into a spiritual slump. Technology is a testing ground of temptation.

Your particular struggles might not intersect with technology, but all of us encounter temptations. When a disciple consistently surrenders to the sins of pride, anger, or lust, to name a few, he or she will feel stuck like a bug to a fly strip.

Jason had zeal for God and aspirations to be a preacher. He struggled with pornography, another sin made very accessible via technology. He battled porn for a while before finally putting down his sword. Surrendering to the same sin over and over and over again will put one in a spiritual slump. What is more, repeated surrender to one sin made my friend vulnerable to all sorts of other temptations he never thought would be tempting. In his slump, he started sexting back and forth with someone at work. He cheated on his wife several times. Eventually, he left her and his kids for another woman. It all started with a present sin that repeatedly got the best of him.

Future fear is another culprit. Fearful anxiety about the future saps spiritual strength. This is, no doubt, why Jesus commands "do not worry about your life" (Matt. 6:25a). This slump starter is subtle, stalking and sneaking up on you like a mountain lion. Once fear of the future has you, it's hard to get out of its grip. Anxiety concerning the future feels like being trapped inside a cinder block room you have built around you one block at a time.

We tend to worry most about things we can't control, manipulate, or influence. Battling future fear showcases our impotence and need for an omnipotent God. And if we lean more into self-reliance than God-dependence, fear, worry, and anxiety will sap our spiritual strength. Fearing the future is a failure of faith. I know that failure like the back of my hand.

One of our kids had a significant health issue surface when he was five years old. Eczema invaded his skin with ferocity. Sometimes it would flare up literally from head to toe. Though he rarely complained, the itch kept him from sleeping well and enjoying the quality of life we envisioned for him.

We took him to doctor after doctor. We tried all kinds of creams to give him relief, which seemed more traumatic for him than the itch! We were totally helpless when it came to helping him. I started to project the current struggle into the future. I imagined bullies poking fun at his eczema. I wondered if he would ever feel comfortable taking off his shirt to swim. Then, my mind wandered off into crazy land. Will eczema keep him from marrying the love of his life and getting the job of his dreams? Will his skin issues throw him into deep and dark depression? I was in an ultimate fight with future fear and ready to tap out. Thankfully,

God showed up to remedy the illness, as he so often does, but not before I wasted so much of my time and energy in debilitating fear.

On our worst days, we feel the weight of worry heavy upon us, like we're carrying a 150-pound barbell on our backs. The accumulative impact of worrying about tomorrow is a spiritual slump. How often do you worry? What do you worry about? Paying the bills, finishing the job, the approval of others, and the flourishing of your kid? If we don't access the grace to faith our fears, we will slump our way out of major league discipleship.

In baseball, there is one slump starter that sends a player out of the major league and into the minors: he can't hit the ball. (The three slump starters for Christians—past regrets, present sins, and future fears—is a three-headed monster that sucks the life out of the soul.) We can't get past the past or persist in the present. We say or sing, "I know God holds the future," but do we really believe it? When we don't, we lose our spiritual swing.

Spinning Wheels

When American Christians become aware that we are stuck in a slump, we tend to do what our rugged individualistic American culture has taught us: we try to pull ourselves up by the bootstraps. When we find the car of our lives stuck in a muddy rut, we step on the gas, pedal to the metal. When we try to get ourselves out of the muddy rut with a "do better" and "try harder" disposition, the tires become more deeply wedged.

If you're thinking, *What can I do to get myself out of the slump*? you're in big trouble. Since we got ourselves into the slump, there's no chance we are going to pull ourselves out of it.

I'm grateful for the Wesleyan holiness tradition that has shaped me. But the quest for holiness loses its beauty when it morphs into moralism. Humanistic moralism takes over when we forget the sovereignty of God and the necessity of his grace, which always comes first to initiate any good change that takes place in us. I bet there were a few times when David thought, *I'd better get my life on the right track to overcome my spiritual slump*. But he didn't. Why? Because he couldn't—not on his own, anyway. You just don't pull yourself out of a slump like the one David was in.

What I love about my Wesleyan tribe is also cause for concern. We have this optimistic view of free will, the human capacity not only for evil but for good. I love the way we theologically refuse to use God as a crutch to do for us what he calls us to do for him: "work out your salvation with fear and trembling" (Phil. 2:12b). But there are times, many, when we need God to do for us what we cannot do for ourselves. What do you do when you find yourself with neither the will nor the power, the willpower, to work yourself out of the slump? What can you do to overcome long-held habits of thinking, doing, and feeling that are contrary to the values of God's kingdom?

Bad habits over time create a rut in the mud, preventing any spiritual traction for the car of your life. You need to be pulled out of the mud, out of the slump, by a force bigger and stronger than you. You need a tow truck of grace.

Try harder! Swing faster! Do better! Rugged individualistic self-sufficiency is never ever the way out of the slump. You may be in a spiritual slump and nothing you try seems to be helping. You still suit up and show up to play the game, but you feel stuck in a slump caused by past regrets, present sins, and/or future fears. Switching metaphors again, your tires are stuck a foot deep in sludge; you're not going anywhere. In order to save face, you hide your quiet desperation behind a plastic smile. You need divine disruption, a tow truck of grace. So did David, and he got one!

Divine Disruption

David's degeneration was divinely disrupted by grace. The tow truck of grace comes in 2 Samuel 12:1–13. Right after 2 Samuel 11 ends with: "But the thing David had done displeased the LORD" (v. 27b), we might expect to read:

"so the Lord gave up on David" or "the Lord destroyed David" or "the Lord thumbed his nose at David." We read instead: "The LORD sent Nathan to David" (2 Sam. 12:1a). That is an odd transition from the end of one chapter to the beginning of a new chapter, from the last sentence of chapter 11 to the first sentence of chapter 12.

"The LORD sent Nathan to David." I used to think this sentence was indicative of the wrath of God. I thought God sent Nathan to punish David for adultery and murder, to stick David's face in his sinful vomit. But I don't think that's the best reading of the text. "The LORD sent Nathan to David" may actually be one of the most beautiful, grace-filled sentences in all of Scripture. "The LORD sent Nathan to David" not because God was out to destroy or give up on David, but to do for David what David couldn't do for David.

Those two sentences together powerfully encapsulate the ugliness of human sin and the beauty of God's grace. It's easy to miss because of the chapter divisions, so let's read them together: "The thing David had done displeased the LORD. . . . The LORD sent Nathan to David." Second Samuel 11 was a very bad chapter in David's story. In 2 Samuel 12, God quite literally wrote a new chapter for David, one that was full of grace.

Even though he had every right to do so, God did not abandon David. And he won't give up on us, even if we have given up on ourselves. When we displease the Lord, like David did, God will do his part to divinely disrupt our degeneration. He will step in to save us from the slump any way he can, sending a tow truck to pull us out of the mud.

As you read David's story up to 2 Samuel 11, when his slump hit a low point, it's rather easy to despair for David. That is, until we remember that David was not a self-made, but a God-made, man. The hope we have is that the God who seemed bent on blessing David will help David conquer his demons. Because of the character of God, we have hope for David, despite the character of David. And, because of the character of God, there's hope for us too.

Let's take a closer look at this grace-filled chapter. In verses 7–12, the prophet Nathan confronts David. We too often view confrontation with suspicion or disdain, but it was a saving grace for David. He needed to be confronted. Confrontation is the only way to stop a runaway train. God, through Nathan, reminds David of all the ways God has blessed him. Then there's this powerful sentence that captures the generous, gracious heart of God so well. God said to David, "And if all this had been too little, I would have given you even more" (2 Sam. 12:8b). It's the garden of Eden all over again: "You are free to eat from any tree in the garden" (Gen. 2:16). God has given David everything.

I mean, *everything*. Yet, David goes after the one thing off-limits to him—a married woman named Bathsheba.

"I would have given you more." (The God we so often displease is the God who is bent on blessing us.) Admittedly, I am so much like David. God has given me everything I could ever want and more. I used to be a shepherd boy with nothing, a high school–dropout alcoholic. Then God made me a king, restoring dignity, bestowing hope, and igniting purpose in my life. Why, then, am I tempted to run after the few things that displease him? Perhaps the better question is: Why does God not run away from me for so quickly and frequently displeasing him?

(Look at the verbs of God. God said to David, "I anointed you . . . I delivered you . . . I gave you" (2 Sam. 12:7–8). Now look at David's verbs, his actions against God. God through Nathan said to David, "you struck down Uriah . . . and took his wife . . . you killed . . . you despised me" (2 Sam. 12:9–10). God blessed David, and David displeased God in the most egregious ways. David despised God. The Hebrew word for despise is *bayza*, which means to accord little value or worth to someone or something. It's the same word used to describe how Goliath despised David (1 Samuel 17:42) and how Michal, David's wife, despised David when he danced before the Lord (2 Samuel 6:16).)

In the same way that David was despised and devalued by Goliath and Michal, David despised and devalued the God who gave him everything. That's what David did. How did God respond? With grace! "The LORD sent Nathan to David" (2 Sam. 12:1a).

Grace upon Grace

The only force strong enough to stop a runaway train like David was grace! When a player is stuck in a slump and sinking fast, someone has to intercede. God sent Nathan to David to stop the bleeding, to disrupt David's degeneration, to begin the process of pulling David out of the spiritual slump.

After being confronted by God's grace through Nathan, David finally came clean: "I have sinned against the LORD" (2 Sam. 12:13a). Well, it's about time! David kept his adultery and murder under wraps for almost nine months. His slump was a soul-destroying secret. He finally acknowledged his sin. Why? God's extravagant grace was a gift that made David aware of the enormity of his sin. This doesn't sound like a gift until we realize that true grace does not end with guilty condemnation but gracious liberation. Grace leads to confession, which results in cleansing.

David endured consequences from his sin, such as dissension and death in his family. But pictured next to the outrageous grace of God the consequences fade into the background. John, describing Jesus, writes: "For of His fullness we have all received, and grace upon grace" (John 1:16 NASB). By and large, David's life is a story of grace upon grace.

"The LORD sent Nathan to David" (2 Sam. 12:1a) . . . grace upon grace!

Nathan said to David, "The LORD has taken away your sin. You are not going to die" (2 Sam. 12:13b) . . . grace upon grace!

The last section of 2 Samuel 12, verses 24–31, doesn't get much attention, but it is chock-full of grace. David and Bathsheba, a couple whose initial coming together was adulterous, were married and had a second child (God called the newborn Jedidiah, which means "loved by the LORD" (see 2 Samuel 12:24–25). Grace upon grace!)

Joab, David's friend and army commander, was out fighting David's battles while the king was bored in his boxers on the rooftop, lusting. Joab led the Israelite army against the Ammonites. He was about to take Rabbah, their royal city. Joab knew that if he took the city victoriously the city would be named after him, since David was nowhere in sight. So, Joab sent word to King David: "besiege the city and capture it" or the city "will be named after me" (see 2 Samuel 12:26–28). Joab preserved David's reputation. A friend like that is a grace upon grace!

David was rusty. He hadn't picked up a sword in a long time. His hands were too full of Doritos, while he binged on Netflix crime shows, to pick up anything else. David put on his armor (which, surprisingly, still fit over his growing beer belly), grabbed his sword, and went off to finish the battle at Rabbah. David's military skills were dormant but present (2 Samuel 12:29–31). He still had it! David was victorious . . . grace upon grace!

Just when we think God has had enough with David, he gives even more to David. More children. More skills. More success. Why does God do that? The answer is simple: grace!

Perhaps the greatest grace of God toward David was one of legacy. The headline hanging over David's head that we remember most is not the one describing his slump: "the thing David had done displeased the LORD" (2 Sam. 11:27b). No, here is the best-known headline about David, in God's words: "a man after [my] own heart" (1 Sam. 13:14). David, despite his sorry slump, is known as one of the most godly kings of Israel. His poetic prayer journal, the Psalms, has been a source of comfort and guidance for billions of slumpers throughout many times and places. Grace upon grace upon grace!

Some of the sorriest spiritual slumpers in the Bible were disrupted by divine grace and experienced miraculous transformation. Jacob tried to outwit anyone who got in his way, even God, until God disrupted Jacob's degeneration with a wrestling angel. Jacob became Israel (see Genesis 32:22–32). Simon degenerated into denial and depression. God disrupted his degeneration with a grace-filled fish breakfast on the beach. Simon became Peter (see John 21). Saul degenerated into persecuting Christians. God disrupted Saul's degeneration with a blinding light on the Damascus road. Saul became Paul (see Acts 9:1–31).

Grace is God's way of disrupting our degeneration to get us out of a slump and back on a streak. You and I are not stuck in the mediocrity of minor league discipleship. God's grace has the power to transform our story.

God Still Sends Nathans

Whether or not you know it, God has likely sent many Nathans your way over the course of your life. This act of grace has the power to change your trajectory in significant ways. Mickey Mantle, the New York Yankees' phenom, experienced the grace of a God-sent Nathan.

Mantle experienced lots of hitting streaks in baseball but big-time slumps in his personal life. He was an alcoholic and a womanizer. He separated from his wife and four kids to pursue his partying and infidelity. He drank so heavily it destroyed his liver. He received a transplant, but the damage was already done to his body. The end was near for Mantle.

Just like God sent Nathan to David, God sent Bobby Richardson to Mickey Mantle. Richardson played for the Yankees with Mantle. They were friends, but led very different lives. Richardson was a Christian and lay preacher. He had shared the gospel with Mantle many times, but it didn't seem to stick. When Mantle experienced major health complications from his degeneration, his long slump, he was ready for God's disrupting grace. The Lord sent Bobby to Mickey. Mickey became a Christian because of the grace of God through Bobby Richardson, a Nathan.

There are many Nathans God uses to lovingly disrupt our degeneration with grace.

Confrontation can be a Nathan. It can come from a believer or unbeliever, friend or enemy, neighbor or stranger. I remember as a young lead pastor being confronted by someone on my staff. During my yearly evaluation of her job performance, I invited her to evaluate my ministry. She did. It stung. But her willingness to point out an Achilles' heel in my ministry probably saved my ministry.

Disappointment is often a Nathan of grace. God doesn't glory in our heartbreak, but he often redeems it to stop the spiritual bleeding. Every job loss, failure, break-up, and let-down, despite and maybe because of the pain, can awaken and revive us in surprisingly fruitful ways.

Discontentment is a Nathan. Have you experienced a loss of pleasure in things that once excited you? Do you feel moody, miserable emptiness? Has the thought ever struck you: *If everything is going so well, why am I so discontent?* This unpleasant sentiment can expose and eradicate the warped priorities that led us into the spiritual slump.

A sermon or Scripture passage can be a Nathan. Both are like a mirror that reveals the wrinkles in your life—not to shame, but to save you.

Not all Nathans sting like the ones previously mentioned, but all have the potential to help. The grace-filled Nathan might be an extravagantly generous, unmerited gift someone gives you. Maybe it's a dream or vision. Perhaps the Nathan is a book, movie, song, or painting that speaks to your soul. Maybe the divine disruption is an event, something that happens to or around you. God might even use a social media post as a Nathan of grace to nudge you out of your slump and back onto a streak again.

How does God disrupt David, me, and you? With the force of grace! Make no mistake about it. If you are spiritually stuck in a slump, God will lovingly hound you with a Nathan. You might be tempted to dismiss, ignore, or run from this Nathan. Don't! God sends a Nathan as a grace to change the trajectory of your life for the better.

The Ultimate Slugger

Zach, my son, was a Little League slugger. He crushed the ball almost every time he came up to bat. Chip off the ole block! He was seven years old then. A machine pitched the ball to the same spot and at the same speed almost every pitch. Zach knew what to expect when he went up to the plate. That changed when he turned eight.

In the 8–10 league, consistent pitching machines were replaced by the erratic pitching of kids. The pitches were as unpredictable as a masterful mystery novel. Kids threw the ball all over the place, mostly at Zach's head. In his first game, with a wobbly armed nine-year-old pitching for the opposing team, Zach was hit with the ball—twice in one game!

My slugger turned into a slumper. Zach became terrified of the ball when he went up to bat. When the pitcher went into his windup, Zach would shuffle back away from the plate. He was too far from the plate to hit a pitch in the strike zone. He was bailing out and swinging the bat half-heartedly. He spent that entire season stuck in a slump.

I remember advising Zach from the bleachers with the rest of the coaching staff, I mean, parents. "Zach, don't bail out. The ball won't hurt . . . that bad. Hang in there, buddy. You've got this." My coaching didn't get Zach out of his slump. I knew Zach could do better. In his first two seasons, he was a slugger. Seeing my son in a slump broke my heart. I recall wishing I could jump into his body and do for Zach what he couldn't do for himself. Unfortunately, that's impossible.

What I couldn't do for Zach, God did for us. The heart of our Father broke due to the spiritual slump of the human race. He saw how stuck we were and knew he made us for something more, something better. God did for us what I couldn't do for Zach. He jumped into our body through the incarnation of Christ, and hit the ball out of the park for us. Jesus was hit by all kinds of nasty pitches. He didn't flinch. He didn't back out. "But he was pierced for our transgressions, he was crushed for our iniquities; the punishment that brought us peace was on him, and by his wounds we are healed" (Isa. 53:5).

Jesus was God's ultimate plan of disrupting our degeneration, of redeeming and restoring what we lost in the fall. By jumping into the sinful slump of the human condition, God paved the way for us to be saintly sluggers.

God didn't just send Nathan to David, he sent Jesus to us!

Candlelight Dinner of Grace

Not long after our honeymoon, I goofed. Amy told me she was going to cook dinner for 6:00 p.m. She taught kindergarten at the time and, somehow, still had the energy to prepare a meal for us after a long day. It was a Friday, my day off from the rigors of ministry. As usual in the fall, I went fly-fishing on my day off.

Five o'clock rolled around, and I knew it was time to head home for dinner at 6:00. But a few more minutes couldn't hurt. At 5:30 I decided to keep on fishing, knowing full well I'd be late for dinner with Amy. Cell phones were becoming popular at the time, but I didn't have one yet. I was going to be late and didn't have a way to call Amy. Honestly, I didn't care that much. I was catching trout after all. Besides, this was my day off, and I could spend it how I wanted. It was 8:00, two hours after I promised to be home, before I pulled into our driveway.

I walked in and saw Amy's worried face. "Where were you?" she asked with concern. "I was so worried about you. I thought you fell in the river and drowned. You said you'd be home by 6:00 and now dinner is ruined. Please call me next time to let me know you're okay," Amy pleaded.

Instead of offering an apology, I dug in my newlywed heels. "How dare you try to limit my hobbies! This is my day off and I can spend it how I please." I stormed out of the house like I was the victim. Yep, I was a dufus!

I went for an hour-long drive to cool off and clear my head. On my way home, I thought of possible excuses and arguments in defense of my degeneration. I totally disregarded Amy's feelings. She worked hard teaching little rascals all day. Despite her exhaustion, she cooked us dinner. I caused her to worry and then acted like she was at fault. Like I said, what a dufus!

Walking up the steps to our cozy apartment, I rehearsed my defensive apology speech. That's when I saw it. Our little deck was decked out with candles all around the perimeter.

The table was covered with a white lace cloth. There were two tall candles on the table, lighting up the new meal Amy had prepared, her second that day. Then my eyes landed on Amy. She looked beautiful.

How did Amy respond to my disregard, defensiveness, degeneration, and dufus-ness? With a candlelight dinner of grace. I fell in love with her all over again. The grace she displayed made me love her more, not less.

Just when we think God is going to dump or divorce us, he shows grace. He disrupts our degeneration, not with retaliation or annihilation, but with a candlelight dinner we don't deserve or expect. He brings us to his banquet table, and his banner over us is love (Song of Songs 2:4). And we exclaim: "Blessed are those who are invited to the wedding supper of the Lamb!" (Rev. 19:9a).

You stumble to your seat at his table, still a bit drunk from the distance between you and God that your degeneration caused. That's when you hear him say, "Take and eat my body broken for you. . . . Take and drink my blood poured out for you . . . do this in remembrance of my love for you" (see Luke 22:19–20). An encounter with that kind of extraordinary grace has the power to tow-truck us out of the spiritual slump!

Reflection

- Which slump starter is most likely to get you down on your worst days—past regrets, present sins, or future fears?

- When and how has God sent a Nathan to divinely disrupt your degeneration and get you out of your slump? Did that Nathan come in the form of confrontation, discontentment, or disappointment? Or was it a sermon, Scripture, song, movie, dream, gift, book, or something else?

- Reflect on the grace upon grace that God extended to David in 2 Samuel 12. In what ways do you relate to David's experience of God's grace?

- Is extravagant grace more likely to become an excuse to sin more and love God less or a reason to sin less and love God more?

Prayer

Lord, thank you for disrupting our degeneration with grace. You send Nathans to us like you did to David. We look back on our lives and see your grace upon grace everywhere. May your grace be for us like a tow truck that gets us out of the muddy rut. We recognize that we are hopelessly stuck in a spiritual slump without your grace. Amen.

| 3 |

DETESTATION

Detestation is being disgusted by what disgusts God. Learning to not only love what God loves but also to hate what he hates is a mark of Christian maturity. God hates the spiritual slump because it hurts us and keeps us from joy-filled holy living. If we don't detest the slump with God-like detestation, we will stay stuck in it longer than we need to . . . maybe forever. The first step out of the slump, as the life of David highlights, is to detest it.

Hate the Slump

To detest means to dislike intensely, to be disgusted with someone or something. What disgusts you? What grosses you out? Here's a list of things I detest: vinegar, pop music, egg salad, the smell of junior high boys at a youth group all-nighter, political news reporting, the Dallas Cowboys, price gouging, and when a person plays with his phone while you pour out your heart to him. What's even more disgusting to me is physical, verbal, and sexual abuse; racial and gender oppression; human trafficking; and corporate corruption. I could go on and on listing things I detest, but I'll spare you.

If only we detested the spiritual slump like I detest the things on my list, it would motivate us out of the slump. After God intervenes to disrupt us with grace, the next step out of the slump is to detest the slump. If the slump does not disgust, it will persist.

A friend asked me to coach Little League baseball for nine- and ten-year-old boys. Obviously, he wasn't a very good friend. I'm not sure what I was thinking or if I was thinking, but I accepted the invitation.

My team made the Bad News Bears look good. The whole team was in a slump pretty much the entire season. There were several games when not a single one of my players got a legitimate hit to get on base. They either struck out, walked, or got nailed by a pitch. Our team would get beat by teams everyone else demolished.

You would think the kids were depressed and demoralized in the dugout. Nope! They were laughing at knock-knock jokes, goofing off, belching, and flatulating with pride. Some of the players were in the habit of leaving the dugout to buy a hot dog or candy at the concession stand—during the game! Why did I say yes to coaching?

The kids didn't seem bothered by their slump at all. They were completely content. We coaches were not. We knew their potential to play better than they did. I wanted to yell at them, "You guys don't deserve to eat hot dogs and laugh in the dugout. How dare you have fun? Most of you haven't touched the ball with your bat in three games. Don't you care that you are losing to a team that every other team destroys?" I held back, but only because parents were watching.

Some of the players—and I use the term loosely— would say to me, "Coach, did you see the foul ball I hit; I crushed it." I'm not making this up! Foul balls don't lead to runs! They were willing to settle for foul balls. There was absolutely no sense of urgency. They were content to stay in the slump, eat junk food, and tell stupid jokes. No matter how hard I tried, I could not make them detest their slump. I wanted them to be disgusted by their habit of not playing to their potential; they were not!

What drove me nuts that year was not that the team was in a slump. Slumps happen. What bugged me was their lack of concern. They didn't care. And, they didn't care that they didn't care. Little League baseball acedia! Their "oh well" attitude and their apathetic complacency were maddening. I wanted to go all Billy Martin on them! (In case you're wondering, Billy Martin was a hot-headed coach for the New York Yankees known more for kicking dirt on umpires than coaching players.)

Once a slump stops bothering ball players, it is the beginning of the end of their career. A player must detest the slump to overcome the slump. A Christian must hate the slump or he/she will stay in it for a long time, maybe forever. He or she will rationalize with, "I never killed anybody; I haven't had an affair; I don't view porn as often as my friends do; I'm a good person." Sounds a lot like a player bragging, "But I really crushed that foul ball." (Euphemizing the slump results in spiritual death.)

Jane is hypercritical of her husband, subjecting him to constant public shaming. She yells at her kids for behaving like kids. She is verbally abusive and loose with other people's secrets. Jane is a Christian. She posts Bible verses often on social media, along with judgmental rants against people who, from her perspective, compromise Christian values. Those who know Jane well see her quite differently than she sees herself. We perceive her to be in a slump. She seems to perceive herself as hitting the ball out of the park, batting a thousand. The human capacity for self-deception and a lack of slump-awareness startles me.

How can someone in a severe spiritual slump not see it? I wonder how many people in the church are in a slump and can't discern its ugliness. "I only struck out four of five at bats today. I got a really nice hit ten games ago." Sometimes the church makes it too easy for disciples to stay in the spiritual slump. The church communicates, with the best of intentions, "God doesn't want you to hate yourself . . . he loves you just the way you are . . . you're saved by God's grace, not your goodness." And all of this is true from my reading of Scripture. But the unintended interpretive spin that results is hazardous to our spiritual health.

God does love us as we are. We are saved by his grace. But God hates sin! He detests sin because it has a historical track record of dehumanizing us humans. Sin chips away at the image of God in us. God most definitely wants us to see the hideousness of sin. He knows that if we embrace or tolerate sin we will stay stuck in a perpetual spiritual slump, often not realizing we're in one.

Repeated sin is like an overplayed song. Sometimes I become head-over-heels in love with a song, usually alternative rock. I play the song over and over and over again until, eventually, I become numb to its sound. When in the spiritual slump, we have a tendency to keep playing the same sins over and over again until we barely notice the sin song we're singing. Habitual sin turns conviction into complacency. This is typical of the spiritual slump.

But God, as we discussed in the previous chapter, will find a way to graciously disrupt the sin song. He will expose its ugliness so that we detest our sin. God's goal is not that we hate ourselves because we love sin, but that we hate our sin because we love God. When we embrace God's grace most fully, we detest our sin most fiercely. That's what King David discovered.

David's Complacency

You would think David knew better. But, somehow, he became so distant from God that conviction was ambushed by complacency. His detestation for sin was hijacked by his denial of sin. His batting average dipped lower and lower, it seems to the point at which he stopped caring. He just threw his hands up and accepted the spiritual slump, singing with Phil Collins, "I don't care anymore." And he did the unthinkable—committing adultery with Bathsheba and murder to cover up the pregnancy.

David was in a slump long before the unthinkable happened. The problem is not so much that he got into a slump; most of us will. The bigger problem was that he didn't acknowledge the slump enough to detest it. So the slump went on and on and on, until he found himself in bed with a married woman not married to him.

I wonder if, before David committed adultery and murder, he said to himself or a friend, "I have never committed adultery or murder. I'm doing okay." The Holy Spirit in us is like a carbon monoxide detector alerting us to dangers we can't see but can kill us. In the same way that the carbon monoxide detector sounds an alarm to warn of colorless, odorless, and toxic gas in our home, the Holy Spirit sounds an alarm to expose the spiritual slump. That alarm is usually more subtle than an annoyingly loud beep. We find ways to ignore the Spirit's alarm. That's why there are so many spiritual fatalities.

Failure to heed the Spirit's warning and detest the slump almost did David in. Almost.

Loving Detestation

For nearly nine months after his sin with Bathsheba and the murderous cover-up, David didn't appear all that remorseful. How does someone who did what David did avoid guilt and remorse? He found ways to keep pushing his degeneration out of his mind. How does one simply get on with one's life after that major debacle? But when the grace of God, through Nathan, divinely disrupted David, the king experienced remorseful disgust.

David wrote Psalm 51 after being confronted by the prophet Nathan. It's a psalm of love and hate, or loving detestation. The gracious love of God is the starting point for Psalm 51. David began with a focus on God's "unfailing love" (v. 1). The Hebrew word is *chesed*. It's a love that goes beyond mere covenantal loyalty. This kind of love is resolute in being generously unconditional, a love that is based more on the character of the giver than that of the recipient. Chesed is the offer of unrestricted tenderness even and especially when it is least deserved. When David was stuck neck-deep in a slump, God was still bent on loving David. That's chesed!

David continued the focus in Psalm 51 on God's love, his "great compassion" (v. 1). *Racham* is the Hebrew word David used for "compassion." It comes from the same root as the word for "womb." Racham is not just a warm fuzzy, an empty emotion. It's an emotion that has physical and relational consequences. Like a pregnant woman who experiences a tight bonding with the child growing inside of her, so God our Father has compassion on us. Think of the pain you feel in the pit of your stomach when you see your child suffer. You experience pain in your bowels, or womb, that moves you to act on your child's behalf. That's how God felt for David. That's racham!

The more David reflected on God's outrageous love, the more disgusted he was with his sin. Psalm 51:1 is all about God's love. But the verses that immediately follow are all about hate. When David was most aware of God's love, he hated his sin most. There was no longer denial of sin: "Wash away all my iniquity and cleanse me from my sin. For I know my transgressions, and my sin is always before me. Against you, you only, have I sinned and done what is evil in your sight. . . . Surely I was sinful at birth, sinful from the time my mother conceived me" (vv. 2–5). An acute awareness of God's radical, incomparable love led David to detest his sinful lack of love for God. Sorrow for sin, though painful, leads to liberation from the guilt and shame that come from sweeping sin under the rug. Perhaps this is what Jesus meant by "Blessed are those who mourn, for they will be comforted" (Matt. 5:4).

David did not detest sin simply because he got caught. Craig was leading a double life. He was a church deacon on Sundays and an adulterer on Fridays. The charade lasted for decades until his wife figured it out. He broke his wife's heart and crushed his kids. Sadness overcame him; he wept often. But he barely offered a heartfelt apology to those he hurt most by his choices. It seemed like he was more sorry that he got caught than he was that he sinned. There's a huge difference between the two.

As a pastor, I have often found myself with broken people trying to pick up the pieces caused by their moral failure. I offer grace, since any one of us can slide into a slump and make ridiculous, out-of-character choices. Every person in that situation is sorry. However, some are sorry that their sin was discovered and others that their sin was detestable. The latter are the ones who, more often than not, get back on the track of redemptive grace.

David didn't detest sin because it damaged his good reputation among the people. What made all of the redemptive difference for David was the focus of his disgust. King David's sorrow when confronted by the prophet Nathan was different from King Saul's sorrow when confronted by the prophet Samuel. When Samuel confronted Saul in 1 Samuel 15, Saul responded: "I have sinned. But please honor me now before the elders of my people and before Israel; come back with me, so that I may worship the LORD your God" (1 Sam. 15:30). Saul was trying to save face. He was more worried about losing his reputation than losing his soul. He wanted to be honored among the people even when he acted dishonorably.

One of Saul's most disgusting qualities was his inability to be disgusted by his sin. One of David's most endearing qualities was the unrestrained disgust he developed for his sinful slump. This, I think, was the major difference between these two leaders that made all the difference in the trajectory of their lives. Both royalties messed up royally. One sunk into the pages of history as a compromiser who never reached his potential, and the other left a legacy by writing poetic prayers to God called psalms. One seems to not even notice his slump and, therefore, stayed in it. The other was absolutely disgusted by his slump and, in time, overcame it.

So, if David did not detest his sin because he got caught or lost his good reputation, why did he detest his sin? (David hated sin because he loved God.) Plain and simple. Again, David did not hate himself because he loved sin. That would lead to the sort of shame that keeps one stuck in a sinful slump. Shame and self-condemnation don't help anyone. The love of God does.

If we hate our sin for any other reason but love, we will become self-centered legalists. The only way out of the spiritual slump is to become so madly in love with the God who madly loves us that we deeply detest our sin. (David hated sin because he loved God. And that's the first step out of the slump after we encounter the disrupting grace of God.)

Breaking Good

Honestly, denial is an easier, less painful road than disgust. When we begin to feel initial disgust, detesting our slump, we are tempted to run and numb the pain in the palace of pleasures. At first, that's what King David did. We are tempted to look for any Bathsheba we can find to distract us from the brokenness we begin to sense. The Bathsheba can be eating, napping, shopping, viewing, scrolling, drinking, overworking—you name it! These escapes might provide short-term relief, but cause long-term destruction. If we access the grace to lean into the brokenness caused by disgust for the slump, we will "grow up in all aspects into Him who is the head, even Christ" (Eph. 4:15 NASB).

The more we glimpse the powerful beauty of God's chesed (unfailing love) and racham (great compassion), the more likely we will overcome the slump and get back on a spiritual streak again. We need a Psalm 51 moment when we are simultaneously and acutely aware of God's love and our sin. It's a love-hate moment. Intensity of love from and for God fuels an intensity of hatred for our sin. This is brokenness.

Breaking Bad is not just a TV show about a chemistry teacher turned drug dealer; it's a reality for many who, when broken, go off the deep end. But, when the love of God is central, there is such a thing as breaking good. In Psalm 51:17, David writes: "My sacrifice, O God, is a broken spirit; a broken and contrite heart you, God, will not despise." The Hebrew word David used twice here for "broken" is *shabar*. The word picture in the ancient Hebrew mind is the grain in the millstone being crushed to burst out the seeds from the hulls. Brokenness brings new life that makes us whole again. Breaking is good!

Brokenness is the wilderness that transformed Hebrew slaves into a holy nation. Brokenness is the gap between crucifixion and resurrection: the three days of disappointment, denial, and disgust that transformed odorous fisherman into apostolic leaders. Brokenness is the act that turned common bread into Christ's body. Brokenness has the potential to transform ordinary slumpers into extraordinary sluggers. That is, if we let the hands of Christ lovingly break us like bread.

No pain, no gain. If you feel sick in your stomach because of your sin, take heart, you are heading in the right direction, out of the slump. If the stench of your sin is nagging at you, so much that you are ready to make necessary changes to grow spiritually, you are heading out of the spiritual slump. (If you find yourself so remorseful that you are beginning to have hypersensitivity to sin again, like you did when you first fell in love with Christ, then you are heading out of the slump.)

Adam Dunn was a superb baseball player for ten years. He averaged thirty-five homeruns per season and hit at least forty homers in a season five years in a row. But then he dropped to eleven home runs, batted .159, and struck out 177 times. Dunn offered no explanation for his struggles. He didn't quit or deny the slump. He detested it and tried everything to get out of his slump, but nothing seemed to work. Ozzie Guillen, who was Dunn's manager with the

White Sox, said the following year, "I love Adam Dunn. He was terrible last year. But he never gave an excuse. After every game, he stood at his locker and took it. I love Adam Dunn."

Perfect Love

If sin leads us to hate ourselves, we are in big trouble. (Self-condemnation, sour introspection, self-absorption, and self-hatred will not help us to overcome the sinful slump. God's loving kindness does not produce a legalistic guilt that leads to despair, but a holy disgust that leads to hope.) The apostle Paul said it best: ("Godly sorrow brings repentance that leads to salvation and leaves no regret, but worldly sorrow brings death" (2 Cor. 7:10).)

I'm not at all against therapy. In fact, I benefitted greatly from counseling when I was in a slump. But if therapy euphemizes sin, it prevents remorse. "You're okay. I'm okay. We're all okay" is hardly a helpful perspective. A therapeutic culture explains away or excuses the sinful slump. Theological convictions, biblically informed and Spirit-inspired, remind us that sin is rather detestable because it does damage to humans. Theology must inform therapy.

Years ago, a friend of mine drove on the shoulder of a road to pass a turning car. When she did, she killed a kid riding his bike. Someone paid the penalty for her lawless act, and she was broken by it. There was no chance she would break that law again. Imagine that something you did literally killed someone. You broke the law, and someone else paid the price with their life. This is the gospel of Jesus Christ.

Our law-breaking did kill someone. My sin and your sin put the God of love on a cross of shame. My sin and your sin have corrupted the cosmos. My sin and your sin is a slap in the face and a spit in the eye of the God who made, knows, and loves us. My sin and your sin put a thick wedge between us and God that nothing but God, through high personal cost, could overcome. My sin and your sin prevent the intimacy we crave with God and people. My sin and your sin chips away at the *imago dei*, the image of God, in each of us. My sin and your sin warp our perceptions of God, self, and others. My sin and your sin blur our vision so that we can't see past the nose on our face to the needs of others and the glory of God.

When we are broken by love, our sin will lead us to say with Isaiah: "I am doomed, for I am a sinful [person]" (Isa. 6:5a NLT); with Paul: "What a miserable person I am! Who will free me from this life that is dominated by sin and death?" (Rom. 7:24 NLT); and with David: "Have mercy on me, O God, according to your [chesed] . . . your [racham] . . . blot out my transgressions. . . . Cleanse me with hyssop, and I will be clean; wash me, and I will be whiter than snow" (Ps. 51:1–2, 7).

The way out of the slump is to view our sin theologically, not therapeutically. Bad therapy might lead us to deny sin while good theology can lead us to detest sin.

One of the problems in the church today is that we have anesthetized the pain of sin. We tend to put lipstick and mascara on sin, giving her a new hairstyle to hide her hideousness. If you pick up and read most any devotional classic written before, say, 1980, what you read will likely elicit disgust for sin that's motivated by the love of God. I triple dog dare you to read Augustine's *Confessions*, Madam Guyon's *Experiencing the Depths of Jesus Christ*, or Oswald Chambers's *My Utmost for His Highest*. Here's an example of what I mean from Chambers: "If we will surrender, submitting to His conviction of that particular sin, He will lead us down to where He can reveal the vast underlying nature of sin. That is the way God always deals with us when we are consciously aware of His presence."[2]

A minimalist view of human sin leads to a minimalist appreciation for God's grace, which leads to minimalist Christian living. When we recognize the enormity of sin's consequences, we will most appreciate the enormity of God's grace. John Wesley believed, experienced, and taught that a deep love from and for God has the power to free us from willful sin. That's perfect love. Love, not legalism or libertinism, pulls us out of the slump.

The Doors asked, "Who do you love?" That's a good question, because who you love will determine what you hate! Because I love the Philadelphia Eagles, I hate when the Dallas Cowboys win. Because I love my grandmother, I hate cancer. Because I love quiet, I hate noise. Because I love the poor, I hate poverty. Because I love honesty, I hate cable news. (If we love God, we will hate sin.)

The more aware we are of God's unconditional, eternal love for us, the more we will love God back. And the more we love God, the more we will hate what he hates. Because God loves us, he hates the sinful slump that keeps us stuck in minor league living. When we detest the slump because we love God, our bats will begin to make solid contact with the curveballs life throws our way.

Reflection

- What do you detest? What is disgusting to you? Have fun naming what grosses you out.
- Is your sin as disgusting to you as the things you named?
- Spend some time on your knees, if possible, slowly reading Psalm 51 aloud. During your first reading, focus mostly on the words and phrases that showcase God's love for you. With God's love for you as the foundation, read Psalm 51 a second time, mourning and detesting your sins because of God's love.

- Reflect on the ways God has loved you lately and throughout your life. What are the tangible expressions of love that God has demonstrated to you? Take your time recounting them.

- Why do you think God hates sin? Of course, God hates sin because he loves us. But what does sin do to us that makes God detest sin so much?

- The next step out of the slump, after God's disrupting grace, is to detest the slump. Do you share God's detestation for the sinful slump? On a scale from 1 to 10, how much do you hate sin? What is the evidence for that rating?

Prayer

Lord, help us to love what you love and hate what you hate. We have become too comfortable with sin, even though we know it has a devastating, dehumanizing impact upon us. Love us out of our sin. Help us to overcome the shame that keeps us stuck in the slump. Liberate us from hating ourselves because we love sin. Convict us so that we hate sin because we love you. Amen.

| 4 |

DISCLOSURE

Disclosure can heal the deep wounds in the soul caused by the spiritual slump. Concealment kills but confession heals. The church is designed by God not merely to be a community where we showcase our victories, but where we share our struggles. Keeping the slump a secret from those who can help us out of it does spiritual, emotional, relational, and even physical damage to us. David discovered freedom and forgiveness when he embraced disclosure, confessing the slump.

Concealment Kills

We have been conditioned by social media to habitually present our ideal self instead of our real self. We conceal our blemishes and wrinkles, our sin, shame, and struggle. The human tendency to hide our weaknesses behind some sort of fig leaf is as old as the garden of Eden. However, the drive for perfection and progress in the twenty-first century is more intense than ever. Let's face it: we are so worried about what others think of us that we airbrush our struggles. For example, most of us know what to say when asked to describe our weaknesses during a job interview. We tell the interviewer: "My greatest weakness is that I'm a perfectionist." And, of course, most employers want employees who are perfectionistic when it comes to job performance. So, this admitted weakness really is a strength.

Clearly, we have a hard time admitting weakness, so we cover it up in various ways. When we do, we limit the transformational work God wants to do in us. If we conceal our imperfections from ourselves and others, there's a good chance we'll try to hide our blemishes from God too. We put up "do not enter" signs in those areas of our lives to keep God and others out. Isolation perpetuates the spiritual slump. Perhaps this is why God asserts at the start of creation: "It is not good for the man to be alone" (Gen. 2:18).

You hardly ever see a Facebook post or Twitter message that admits: "I sinned today and hate it," or "Just cheated on my taxes" or "Lied to my spouse four times this week" or "Gossiped about a friend and feel sorry" or "Got high last night." Actually, I have seen that last post a few times. Please don't get me wrong. I'm not advocating that you air your dirty laundry on social media. Please don't. No one wants that. I'm simply making the point that admitting weakness is difficult for us. We learn as children ways to present our ideal self and not our real self. We take this into adulthood, and it does significant damage to our relationships with God and people.

The church can be a secret society. The social media mentality is totally antithetical to Christian community. Presenting our Sunday best, our airbrushed self, in the context of Christian fellowship, prevents us from experiencing the beauty of genuine community. I'm not suggesting that we in the church are a formal secret society, like the Freemasons. (I am noting that the church is all too often a society of secrets, where people struggle alone in silence.)

Why do Christians struggling, perhaps with addiction, feel that the safest place to bare their naked soul is within an anonymous recovery group? Why are we so quick to conceal our Saturday worst by wearing our Sunday best? The church should be the first and safest place to confess our slump.

Yet, concealment of the slump happens all the time in the church. Why is it that the one place on earth where people should feel most free to confess our slump, the church, is often the last place people tend to come clean?

Secret sin sabotages the soul. I'm so quick to criticize politicians and the news media for cover-ups, but I, too, am guilty of concealment. Christians who want to live for God but find themselves engaged in secret sin, struggle, or shame are in a slump. When the secret stays secret, it eats away at the soul like a cancer until the soul is completely gone.

Some blame their slump on hypocrisy in the church. Others blame their slump on theological doubts. But as far as I can tell, many who are in a slump are stuck because they have concealed their struggles. There are serious consequences that result from concealment. Concealment kills. Concealment kills us physically, emotionally, relationally, and spiritually. Concealment kills the body, mind, and relationships. Concealment kills the soul.

Consequences of David's Cover-Up

David learned the hard way that concealment kills. He described the damage that results from covering up sin in Psalm 32. He reflected back on his sin with Bathsheba and his murderous concealment. Concealment, in that case, literally killed Uriah, Bathsheba's husband. But it nearly killed David too.

David noted how concealment damaged his body and soul in Psalm 32:3–4: "When I kept silent, my bones wasted away through my groaning all day long. For day and night your hand was heavy on me; my strength was sapped as in the heat of summer." There were physical ramifications David endured because he kept silent, refusing to confess his sin. His bones wasted away. That sounds painful. David felt the convicting hand of God heavy upon him. Deep conviction is as comfortable as walking barefoot on hot coals. When we respond to conviction with concealment, we experience the physical and emotional depletion that David suffered. "My strength was sapped," he recalled.

For almost nine months, David concealed his sin. For much longer than that, he kept his slump a secret, maybe even from himself. This decision adversely impacted every part of David—mind, body, and soul. Bottling up sin does damage from the inside out. Concealment kills.

Fig Leaves

The temptation to conceal, cover up, and hide are ancient. Adam and Eve tried to conceal their sin. They hid their true self behind the fig leaves of the false self. Social media can be a contemporary fig leaf through which we hide our true self behind our false self.) I imagine Adam and Eve posting on Facebook: "Had an awesome day eating fruit in the garden of Eden," with pictures of Cain and Abel when they were young and still cute. Hashtag "blessed."

We use the fig leaves of appearance, ability, and accomplishment to cover our insecurity, inadequacy, and inferiority. Fig leaves, we think, hide our slump from God, others, and even ourselves. But fig leaves are biodegradable. Life has a way of shredding the self-sufficient leaves to reveal our naked God-dependence. The bottom line is that the fig leaves we wear prevent the intimacy we crave. Why? Because it keeps God and people from getting to the real person behind the ideal.

David knows the pain that comes with concealing sin. We do too. When we keep the slump a secret, it can cause ulcers, depression, and fatigue. Withholding confession hurts. The constipation of unconfessed sin wreaks internal havoc. Perhaps this is why the New Testament intimates a connection between sin and illness. The disciples asked Jesus about the blind man: "Who sinned, this man or his parents?" (John 9:2). Now, we know that many people experience physical infirmity not because of their personal unconfessed sin but because we live in a fallen world corrupted by sin. But, I'm convinced there are people with ulcers and other illnesses who are sick because of confession constipation or, if you prefer, concealed sin, struggle, and shame.

David suggested that the longer the disease of concealed sin stays in you, hiding below the surface, the more damage it will do to every area of your life. God knows this, so he will smother us with loving conviction.

God is the cosmic Interrogator who tries to squeeze a confession out of us. That's what I think David was getting at when he wrote to God: "your hand was heavy on me" (Ps. 32:4). God gets heavy-handed when it comes to removing our fig leaves to reveal our naked need for him. God probes, questions, and convicts us so that a confession comes out of us.

Since we're talking about confession, I confess to watching too many shows featuring law enforcement. *Law and Order*, *CSI*, and *Criminal Minds* are among my favorites. If you're judging my taste in TV shows, be sure to confess that. Practically every episode in each of these shows features an interrogation room scene. The interrogation room is the place where hard questions are asked by officers and complete honesty is demanded of the suspect. I just love watching the criminal squirm!

God is the ultimate Interrogator. He probes. He squeezes. He convicts. This doesn't gel with popular images of God as a gracious white-bearded grandfatherly type or a gregarious encouraging endorser. We assume God exists to make us happy, but that's a farce. God's aim is not primarily to make us happy but to make us holy, so that holiness becomes our happiness. Truth be told, sometimes God has to make us unhappy to make us holy. He will lay his hand "heavy on [us]," to use David's interrogation language. God might even allow us to sense his absence or that his favor has left us. He helps us to feel the misery of the slump we're trying to conceal. He wants to bring the secret slump to the surface and get us to talk. God will play bad cop if he has to, but only because he is good.

Confession Heals

The police or FBI interrogator wants a confession in order to incarcerate the suspect. God, on the contrary, wants our confession to liberate us from our incarceration. God knows that when the words of confession are released, the guilt will be too. Words and guilt are somehow tied together. God wants our liberation, not our incarceration! Concealment incarcerates the Christian. But as soon as we confess, God is like, "Okay, you're free to go and sin no more." This was where David went with Psalm 32. After describing how concealment kills, he shifted to how confession heals.

In Psalm 32:5, David described the outcome of his confession: "Then I acknowledged my sin to you and did not cover up my iniquity. I said, 'I will confess my transgressions to the LORD.' And you forgave the guilt of my sin." David finally refused to cover up his sin with fig leaves. He stopped hiding behind the power of the throne. He was done covering up and came clean.

David confessed it all. I mean everything. There are three different Hebrew words for infractions used in this one verse, which are translated *sin*, *iniquity*, and *transgression*. David confessed it all. He confessed sins against God and others. He confessed the big sins and little sins. He likely confessed sins of commission and sins of omission. He came clean about the "lust of the flesh, the lust of the eyes, and the pride of life" (1 John 2:16). I can almost hear David confess every sin, iniquity, and transgression he could recall: "and then there was that time in third grade when I cheated on the Hebrew language test and didn't tell my priest . . . when I stole my dad's camel to go joy-riding with my pals . . . when I exaggerated the size of the lion I killed."

When David came clean, his guilt was lifted. He said to God, "you forgave the guilt of my sin" (Ps. 32:5b) That's odd. I had to read it many times to see it. God does not just remove the penalty of sin, he takes away the guilt from sin. That's where the healing comes. It's the guilt that tends to get us. Guilt can keep us down, even after we're forgiven. God doesn't just forgive sin, he eradicates guilt. But how does God do it?

To Each Other

When we confess our sinful slump to God, he removes the penalty for sin. But, often, the guilt persists until we confess our slump to another person. Confessing our sins to another sinner is guilt-liberating. It's the remedy that heals us from the deepest wounds caused by shame. That's exactly what James 5:16a boldly claims. James asserted: "Therefore confess your sins *to each other* and pray for each other so that you may be healed" (emphasis added). I have a habit of putting the "that you may be healed" part with the "pray for each other" part. The praying accomplishes the healing, so I thought. But that's not what James 5:16 says. Prayer to God alone doesn't result in healing; it's prayer to God *plus* confession to others that brings healing.

"Confess your sins to each other . . . that you may be healed." Make no mistake about it. James is saying that our healing and the healing of others is directly tied to our confession capacity. Just like it's easy to change the TV channel when those child poverty commercials come on, we tend to channel surf past the "confess your sins to each other" to the "pray for each other" channel. Why? Because confessing our sins to another person is hard. It requires a willingness to take off our fig leaves, our ideal but false self, to let another person see our real, true self.

I was raised in a nominal Roman Catholic family. That was the only option for South Philadelphia Italians like me. I attended Catholic school, but I rarely went to church. People had a name for me. I was a "Chreaster," meaning I only attended church on Christmas Eve and Easter. There are several things I remember from my Catholic upbringing. One is that incense smells awesome. It made Mass more delightful. Another thing I recall is that Catholics recognize the necessity of disclosure, of confessing sins to another person.

Catholics, at least devout ones, go to the confessional weekly, usually on Saturday to prepare for the Sunday Mass. Here's how it works. You go into the confessional booth. There is a wall with a frosted window that separates you from the priest, so he can't identify you. You confess your sins, as many as you can remember. My list was long, especially when I entered the early teen years. After hearing my confession, the priest would mumble a few sentences faster than an auctioneer. At first, I had no idea what he said. In time, I came to realize that my words of confession where met with his words of absolution. The message I got, through somewhat unintelligible speech, was: "You are forgiven."

When my words of confession were met with words of grace, something happened. Verbally disclosing my sin to another person led to the sweetness of liberation, freedom from guilt. My confessing words followed by the priest's gracious words did something to me. Words matter. Concealed sin elicits guilt. Confessed sin induces grace.

Confessing your spiritual slump to another person is not only a Catholic practice, it's a Wesleyan thing too. John Wesley organized five to seven people into groups called bands. The bands met every week for confession, accountability, and support. Wesley believed disciples are not made in isolation, but in community. In the band, confession was not made behind a frosted window of anonymity. Nope! Nor was confession offered to one other person. Band members confessed their sins openly to a group. Before there were anonymous recovery groups, there was the Wesleyan band. You've heard of extreme sports. Well, the band was an extreme small group, certainly not for wimps.

John Wesley wrote his guiding rules for the band on December 25, 1738. You have to be pretty hard-core to do that sort of thing on Christmas Day. Perhaps that is why he was pejoratively called a "Methodist." He wrote: "The design of our meeting is, to obey that command of God, 'Confess your faults one to another, and pray one for another, that ye may be healed.'" One of the rules Wesley articulated was, "To speak each of us in order, freely and plainly, the true state of our souls, with the faults we have committed in thought, word, or deed, and the temptations we have felt, since our last meeting." Here are the ice-breaker questions to start the band meeting: "What known sins have you committed since our last meeting? What temptations have you met with?"[3] Like I said, the band was an extreme discipleship sport.

In Roman Catholic and Methodist traditions, disciples were encouraged to disclose their sin and struggle every single week. Not more than seven days could pass before you came clean to another person or group. There is much wisdom in the practice of confession. It is perfectly designed to help one overcome and avoid the spiritual slump. It's hard to stay stuck in the slump for long when you have a person or group in the know, offering grace and accountability.

Find a Hitting Coach

David practiced confession to God. He did this through his prayer journal called the Psalms. The honest, heartfelt, and angst-filled journaling of confessional prayers to God in the midst of a spiritual slump can be very beneficial. Prayer journaling is the practice of being brutally honest to God about yourself. But, as we've discovered, something more is needed, not necessarily for the forgiveness of sin, but for the freedom from guilt. That something more is confession to a person or group.

Why is it easier for us to confess our sins to a sinless God than it is to confess our sins to other sinners? If God knows about our slump, who cares if people know? When was the last time you disclosed your sins out loud so that God, you, and another person could hear the words? Weeks, months, years, decades, maybe never? The longer you are silent about your slump, the more the guilt eats away at your soul, mind, and body. Confession constipation is painful!

Every slumping ball player needs the help of a hitting coach. The coach monitors a player's swing during the game. He gives advice on adjustments to make when necessary between at bats. He also oversees the player's performance during cage sessions and pregame batting practice. Basically, the hitting coach does two things: he helps the player to diagnose the reasons for the slump and offers tools to guide the player out of the slump.

The slumping disciple needs a coach, too, someone who can absorb confession, analyze the reasons for the slump, and explore tools for overcoming the slump. This coach can take many forms. Here are some.

In my senior year of college, a small congregation fifteen minutes off campus called me to be their pastor. Yes, they were desperate. Most of the people in this small congregation were three times my age. What could someone like me, in my early twenties, tell them that they didn't already know from walking with the Lord for so long? The daunting challenge of pastoring this flock led me to seek support and accountability. I knew I had some growing up to do. I needed a confessor. And I found one.

I asked a college buddy named Rick, who was also called to be a pastor, to meet with me every two weeks. We trusted each other totally. We both needed someone to whom we could confess anything. Like David, we confessed it all—sins, iniquities, and transgressions. I'm convinced this practice kept me from some of the inevitable slumps that plague many young pastors. Rick was my accountability partner, my hitting coach, at that stage in my life.

Five years into pastoral ministry, I went to seminary. In year two, I descended slightly into a slump. It wasn't the seminary's fault. The busyness of full-time graduate studies and part-time pastoring became an excuse for not "inquiring of the Lord." And, as we saw with David, a lack of inquiry leads to a lack of intimacy. I was sinking fast and needed a hitting coach.

I felt nudged, I think by God, to approach my spiritual formation professor and ask for his help. Reg was one of those professors who loved God vibrantly with both head and heart, or as Charles Wesley put it, with "knowledge and vital piety: learning and holiness combined."[4] There were some things I needed to confess, and the guilt was eating away at me. At the first monthly mentoring meeting with

Reg, I chickened out. I thought so well of him, I didn't want him to think less of me. So, I concealed my slump.

During our second meeting, confession got the better of me. I "wept bitterly" (Luke 22:62) like the apostle Peter after disowning Jesus as I poured out my sin, shame, and struggle—my slump—to Reg. By the time I got everything off of my chest, I was a mess. Tears mixed with snot poured down my face. The "I've got it all together" mask was definitely off. No more fig leaves. Then, Reg did something I will never forget. Instead of being disgusted by the naked mess of me, he moved his chair closer. Sitting right in front of me, a foot away, he put his hands on my shoulders. He looked into my tear-filled eyes, when they were not staring at the floor in shame, and offered words of grace: ("Lenny, in the name of Jesus Christ, you are forgiven.")

When my words of confession were followed by Reg's words of grace, the spiritual healing began. In ways I can't explain or quantify, that experience of confession and grace initiated my movement out of the slump and got me back on a streak again. My hitting coach during that slumpy season was a spiritual mentor.

The church I pastored in Northeastern Pennsylvania launched a Celebrate Recovery Program. Our primary goal was to become a healing place for people battling addiction to drugs, alcohol, or gambling. We had no idea that God would use this ministry to not only rescue unchurched addicts, but to raise slumping Christians from death to life. About half of the people who attended Celebrate Recovery came from within our congregation, while the other half came from programs outside of the church such as Narcotics Anonymous (NA), Alcoholics Anonymous (AA), and Gamblers Anonymous (GA). Those in addiction recovery were shockingly quick to confess their failures to the rest of the group. People from the church, ironically, were not used to this unreserved, unfiltered disclosure of struggle in a group setting. Addicts on the road to recovery resist the temptation to mask their struggles. They refuse to present their best self and, instead, present their real self, warts and all. I watched in awe as confessions from friends in the recovery community compelled longtime churchgoers to remove their masks and openly share their struggles.

Amazing grace happened! Disciples stopped concealing and started confessing their sins to each other. People began to open up and come clean about their jealousy, eating disorders, judgmental legalism, anxiety, codependency, and sex addiction. I saw stagnant, slumping Christians come alive. What did it? Not merely confessing their sins to God in prayer, but confessing their sins to each other in community. For those longtime disciples in a spiritual slump, this Christ-centered recovery group became their hitting coach.

Confession is the chemo that kills the cancer caused by concealment. Find a hitting coach. It can be an accountability partner, mentor, small group, counselor, spiritual director, or pastor. Your spiritual life depends on it.

Reflection

- How has your engagement with social media impacted your capacity to present your real self instead of your ideal self?
- Why is it easier for us to confess our sins to a sinless God than it is to confess our sins to sinful people?
- Does your local church provide the safety and space for people to follow the guidance of James who wrote: "confess your sins to each other" (James 5:16)?
- Think of a time when you came clean to a person about a sin or struggle. Did that person offer grace to overcome your guilt? Or did that person shame you?
- Step 4 of Alcoholics Anonymous entails doing a searching and fearless moral inventory of ourselves. Spend some time on your personal moral inventory (PMI). Which two to three wrongs are currently causing you the most guilt and shame?
- Step 5 of AA entails admitting to God, ourselves, and another human being the exact nature of our wrongs. All of us need a hitting coach to help us

out of the slump. A hitting coach is a small group, accountability partner, mentor, spiritual director, pastor, or counselor to whom you can confess your slump. Who can serve as your hitting coach? Who can receive your words of confession regarding the wrongs causing you the most debilitating guilt? Now, schedule a meeting with your hitting coach. You'll be so glad you did.

Prayer

Lord, we recognize that concealment kills but confession heals. Empower us to take off the fig leaves to present our true self to you and others in place of our false self. Give us the courageous audacity to disclose our secret slump, to "be naked and unashamed" (see Genesis 2:25) in the context of Christian community. Lead us to a hitting coach to whom we can confess our slump and receive grace. Amen.

| 5 |

DECISION

(*Decision* is an intentional resolution to do what needs to be done.) One of the ways to combat the gravitational drift into a slump is to decide, in advance, what practices you will engage to get and stay spiritually fit. Doing nothing is a sure way to stay stuck. Some of us need to make basic decisions to get back on track. Others may need drastic decisions to get out of a slump and onto a streak. David committed to a series of decisions, basic and drastic, to get on a spiritual streak and stay there.

Basic and Drastic

When I was eleven, I made the baseball all-star team. The best players from the six other teams in the league were picked for this special crème de la crème team. By some miracle, I was one of them. I started off the season well enough, looking like I belonged there, until I found myself in a hitting slump. The coach began to move me further and further down the batting order from the third to the seventh slot. When you're in a slump, the ball seems entirely too small to hit, pea-sized even. I was struggling with insecurities caused by the slump that only made it worse.

During my Little League nosedive, something odd happened to me while walking home from school with my older sister, Tammy. We were verbally assaulting each other, which wasn't the unusual part. Then, out of nowhere, I felt something wet drop on my head. I touched it and looked at the substance now on my hand. It was a mixture of white and green. I made the mistake of smelling it. It was, as I suspected, pigeon poop! A pigeon dumped on my head. What's worse than a baseball slump? A pigeon digesting on your head while you're in a slump!

I ran all the way home, about ten city blocks, and almost scrubbed my head bald. My mom tried to comfort me with a silver lining in the greenish white junk. She promised: "You know, it's good luck when a pigeon poops on your head."

"Yeah, right, Mom! That's a lie!" I snapped.

She assured me that something good was around the corner for me because of what that bird dropped on my curly, over-gelled hair.

I had a game that very night with the all-star team. With the top of my head still sore from being scrubbed so hard, I put on my batting helmet and stepped up to the plate. The bases were loaded. I felt demoralized, not just from my slump, but from the pigeon fiasco. The pitch came and I swung as hard as possible, I think with my eyes closed. Contact! I crushed the ball. It was a line drive to the opposite field. Going, going, gone! The ball dropped just barely over the right field fence. I didn't just hit a home run but, with the bases loaded, a grand slam! This was the first and last grand slam I would hit in my baseball career. I'll never forget it.

I came out of my slump in style. I credited the turnaround to my good luck charm, the pigeon. More specifically, the feces. My mom was right. What I viewed as gross misfortune was, to my surprise, good fortune. Whenever I found myself in a slump again, I would run under pigeons, hoping one would drop the lucky charm on me. Seriously. I know it sounds crazy—and disgusting. But a player who detests the slump will make any decision necessary to overcome the slump. I swallowed my pride and ran under pigeons because I thought it might transition me from slumper to slugger. Wouldn't you do the same if you were in my cleats?

Mike Schmidt, the Hall of Fame third baseman for the Philadelphia Phillies, said, "When it was really going bad, even in the prime of my career, if you had told me that I would have a better chance of hitting with my back to the pitcher, I would have tried it. You'll do anything to get out of a slump."[5] Would you do anything to get out of a slump?

I stopped believing in good luck a long time ago, but I'm convinced that basic and drastic decisions are necessary to overcome the spiritual slump. Most self-aware ball players realize that decisions are required to go from slump to streak. The decisions could be drastic like: "I will run under pigeons daily" or "I will try to hit the ball with my back to the pitcher." The decisions could be more basic. Getting back to what made you a slugger in the first place can prove beneficial: "I will hit one hundred balls daily" or "I will do arm workouts three times per day to power my swing" or "I will watch and evaluate my hitting video from the previous game like I did during my banner rookie season."

The player, or disciple, who wants out of the slump will courageously make basic or drastic decisions that have positive potential. Albert Einstein has been credited with saying, "Insanity is doing the same thing over and over again and expecting different results." Another way of putting it is: if you do what you've been doing, you will get what you've been getting. New decisions must be made, but it often takes an iron will.

David's Will

God will find a way to *disrupt* our *degeneration* so that we *detest* and *disclose* the slump. God graciously initiates the process that moves us from slump to streak. He does the heavy lifting. Always. But if we don't make *decisions* in response to God's action, we will stay stuck in the slump.

David knew that his resolve mattered. He made a pact with God, a resolution really. We find it in Psalm 101. I call this psalm "David's Will" because he wrote "I will" eleven times in eight verses. He wrote this psalm when he began his rule as king at the age of thirty. These holy decisions were devised to guide his heart, his house, and his kingdom. Regarding his heart, David wrote "I will be careful to lead a blameless life. . . . I will have nothing to do with what is evil" (vv. 2a, 4b). He made some decisions about his household too: "I will conduct the affairs of my house with a blameless heart" (v. 2b). David also determined to govern the kingdom well: "I will put to silence all the wicked in the land; I will cut off every evildoer from the city of the LORD" (v. 8).

Psalm 101, David's Will, lists basic and drastic decisions that were intended to keep David on a spiritual streak. As we know by now, David strayed far from these premeditated decisions with premeditated adultery and murder. These decisive commitments, however, were like a compass to him. After his miserable failure, he recommitted himself to these decisions that once made him a spiritual slugger.

David is not the only character in the biblical story who made major decisions in response to God's grace. Joshua is another. The book of Joshua concludes with a summary of God's grace in establishing his people in the land of Canaan, "flowing with milk and honey" (Ex. 3:17). Joshua responded to God's grace with a will of his own: "But as for me and my household, *we will* serve the LORD" (24:15b, emphasis added). Joshua makes a basic, but important decision.

Zacchaeus's decision in response to God's grace was much more radical. As a tax collector, he got rich by cheating his own Jewish people. He robbed others, which robbed himself of the blessings of God. Then, grace showed up. Jesus graciously offered Zacchaeus the gift of friendship. Jesus said to him, "I must stay at your house today" (Luke 19:5b). This was a big deal since most peasant Jews hated Zacchaeus for overtaxing them. Zacchaeus was shocked by the warmth of Jesus. In response to God's grace, he made a will like David did: "If

I have cheated anybody out of anything, *I will* pay back four times the amount" (Luke 19:8, emphasis added). This drastic decision would likely drain all of Zacchaeus's wealth so that he became like the peasant Jews he had been exploiting. That's over the top!

"Life-Altaring" Decisions

The way out of the slump is to make radical "all or nothing" decisions in response to God's grace. These decisions reflect the deepest longings God has placed within you, deeper than surface desires for self-satisfaction, self-preservation, and self-glorification. What decisions can you make today that reflect your deep-down desire to embrace the God-filled life? What decisions will foster, to put it in the words of a Eugene Peterson book title, "a long obedience in the same direction"? What decisions can you make that flow out of and align with your Christ-centered core values? What decisions can you make that reflect the congruence of your behaviors with your beliefs?

I'm inviting you to devise your own Psalm 101, your will, that fosters "life-altaring" decisions. I know what you're thinking: *This poor guy can't spell worth a lick. It's life-altering, dummy!* No, I actually mean life-altaring. Since life-altering decisions are made at the altar, I'm simply making up a new word. When you make decisions in your heart to offer your best to God, your heart becomes an altar where your life is drastically altered.

The altar of decision is where the rubber meets the road, where push comes to shove, where your love for God is given tangible expression. The altar is decision time, when you put your money or time where your mouth is. The altar is not the place for good intentions or well-articulated beliefs. It's a place where you put up or shut up. As I noted in a previous chapter, we are shaped by the accumulation of little and big decisions we make over a lifetime. (Or, more simply, the decisions we make today determine the person we become tomorrow.)

If degeneration into bitter grudge-holding has initiated your slump, a life-altaring decision will entail offering forgiveness to the one who has hurt you. If degeneration into lust has caused your slump, a life-altaring decision might include installing Internet accountability software on all of your devices. If degeneration into greed has triggered your slump, your life-altaring decision could be to give 15 percent of your income away to people in need or the ministries that serve them. If degeneration into addiction to drugs or alcohol has instigated your slump, one life-altaring decision might be to check yourself into a ninety-day rehab instead of a thirty-day detox center. The slump can smother you and seem impossible to overcome, but you are only one life-altaring decision away from moving toward the streak.

Holy devotion dissipates when it doesn't translate into holy decisions. But when our internal devotion to God does lead to external life-altering decisions for God with our time and money, relationships and vocation, and in public as well as in private, we will soon find ourselves hitting the ball out of the park.

Married couples know that devotion without decision diminishes devotion. So, the slumping couple will put away the phone in the evening, power off the TV, look into each other's eyes, and share the details of their day. They might even decide to go out on a date every Saturday to cultivate intimacy. In order to get past the self-absorption that can destroy their relationship, they might also decide to serve people in need weekly at the homeless shelter, church, or food pantry. This couple will, in time, start hitting the ball with the sweet spot of the bat. Decisions deepen devotion.

Life-altering decisions are not based on pleasure. That's libertinism. Life-altering decisions are not built on guilt. That's legalism. Life-altering decisions are grounded on devotion. That's love. The disciples who make it out of the spiritual slump avoid graceless legalism and cheap grace libertinism.

Batting Practice

The best ball players commit to decisions that become habits. Don Mattingly, the Yankee great, decided he would take batting practice daily. He swung his bat at 250 pitches every single day! He was ready for game day! Small decisions can, over time, have huge consequences. Mattingly is one of the best sluggers to ever play baseball. The daily decisions he made when no one was looking made him a great player.

Dallas Willard, in his book *Spirit of the Disciplines*, explores the Christian equivalent of batting practice. He notes how so many of us want to do the great things Jesus did in ministry. Willard suggests that if we are going to do the great things Jesus did, we have to do what Jesus did before he did those extraordinary things. Jesus spent time with God, his Father, cultivating the kind of intimacy that enabled Jesus to crush the ball spiritually. Jesus' version of batting practice was engaging in decisive habits, or spiritual disciplines, such as prayer, fasting, and solitude. These practices readied him for game day.

When I was in my nasty spiritual slump several years back, the grace of God led me to some very basic life-altaring decisions. The batting practice that prepared me for game day is what I call the J.E.R.C. Plan. Not the best name, I know, but it's easy to remember.

The "J" stands for the practice of journaling. Every week, usually on Monday, I would prayerfully pour out my heart to God on paper through my pen. It was a place for me to be honest to God about everything—my pain, disappointment, frustration, and slump. What came off of my pen often surprised me, coming from places so deep within me I didn't even know the words were there. The Holy Spirit–inspired words that came off my pen often led me to healing places of grace.

The "E" is for examen. At the end of each day, while lying in bed, I would engage in the simple prayer of examen. I adapted this flow for my daily prayerful reflection—*recall* the day, *rejoice* in what God did, *repent* for the ways I didn't attend to God or others, *request* from God what I need most, and *resolve* to love and live well tomorrow. Daily examen enables us to deal prayerfully with today, so we don't experience a spiritual hangover tomorrow. This bedtime prayer forces reflection in ways that are life-giving. Reflection each day keeps the devil at bay.

The "R" is for retreat. If you're like me, it takes you a day or two to get focused and centered in Christ. Retreating annually for two to three days of silence and solitude can do wonders for a slumping soul. Find a monastery, a campground, or a cabin. Enjoy being with God. Cry, laugh, sing, pray, read, nap, hike, then nap some more. Be with God. Attend to the God who attends to you. I promise, you will be refreshed.

The "C" is for community. The first three can be done alone with God. Community is a decision to include others in your quest to journey deeper into Christ, the Savior of slumpers. Consider engaging in community monthly. I emphasized the importance of community in the last chapter, but it bears repeating. I'm strategically redundant (at least, that's what I tell myself). Meet with a mentor, pastor, counselor, spiritual director, or accountability partner. Shoot, meet with all of them one-on-one monthly if you can! Find people who walk with God, who can help you identify the contours of God's grace in the story of your life. The decision to meet monthly with wise, caring people pulled me out of an abysmal spiritual slump. We all need a hitting coach or two.

Will you decide to work the J.E.R.C.? Decide to journal weekly, examen daily, retreat annually, and commune monthly. These basic life-altaring decisions can become a means of grace that decreases the power and length of your slump.

Step Out on a Limb

There's a good chance that you will want to make not only basic, but drastic, life-altaring decisions, especially if you've been in a slump for a long time. Drastic decisions are risky, maybe even downright ridiculous from a purely human perspective. But these adventurous decisions are often necessary to pry us free from our attachment to the safety of status quo, the pursuit of comfort and convenience, that likely led to our slump in the first place.

The older I get, the more inclined I am to be a tree-hugger. When I was in my twenties, I was a bold risk-taker. If God called me to say or do something, to step out on a limb of faith, more often than not, I would. At that point, I really had nothing to lose. But in my late thirties and early forties, there was a magnetic pull toward playing life safe. In midlife we have more to lose. I have a mortgage, a track record of ministry fruitfulness, a reputation, a wife, three kids, a dog, and a cat. I am halfway toward retirement and don't want to do anything crazy. So, instead of stepping out on a limb of faith, I am tempted to play it safe and hug the trunk of the tree. This tree-hugging tendency was a major contributor to my spiritual slump. Why? Because we experience the presence and power of Christ most profoundly not when we cling to the trunk, but when we're out on the limb.

What does a drastic, limb-walking, life-altering decision look like? Our friends hit midlife and made a drastic decision to adopt a teenage boy from Africa. This was an expensive risk for this couple involving lots of time, three years of paperwork, and money, about half a year's salary. They went back and forth from Africa, cutting through lots of red tape, all while trying to care for their three biological children and keep up with their jobs. This was a stressful and risky adventure, but one that enlivened their faith. They decided to be limb-walkers not trunk-huggers, and it made all the difference.

Then there's Charlie. He was a longtime churchgoer who seemed spiritually dry. He was well past midlife when I met him. One day, Charlie encountered a group of homeless people loitering outside of his favorite hardware store. He avoided them, taking the long way around them into the store. This happened a couple of times before Johnnie, one of the homeless guys, struck up a conversation with Charlie. Then, in no time, they became the best of friends. Charlie felt compelled in his late sixties to do something to help his homeless friends who lived in the woods behind our local Walmart.

I recall the weekend Charlie recruited about ten handy people from our church, purchased a bunch of building materials, and went into the woods to build shelters for his homeless friends. He wasn't sure about township regulations, but he took the risk anyway. Love is costly and risky, but worth the risk. As Charlie stepped out on a limb, out of his comfort zone, I saw his life change. God raised him from the spiritual death of the slump. And it took a drastic life-altering decision for Charlie to encounter and embrace grace.

I'm not suggesting you adopt a child or start a homeless ministry. Whether you mentor an at-risk kid, intentionally move into a high-crime area to build relationships, leave a well-established church to plant a congregation in an urban area, initiate a hard conversation toward reconciliation, go on mission to a third-world country, or give an exorbitantly generous gift to someone in need, do *something*. Make a drastic, life-altaring, out-on-a-limb decision. More often than not, God will use this to initiate your movement out of the slump.

In Matthew 25:14–30, Jesus told a story about risk-taking. It's called the parable of the talents. A talent was a sum of money in the ancient world. Three people in the story received different sums to invest. Two of these characters took a risk by investing the money. They were limb-walkers. The third guy was risk-averse and buried the loot safely in the ground. He was a tree-hugger. Jesus told the story in a way that made the play-it-safe guy out to be a faithless villain. Jesus, I'm convinced, told this parable to assert he'd rather us take a drastic life-altaring risk for God's glory and humanity's good, even if we fail, than to never take a risk at all. Riskless living is deadly for disciples.

Amy and I have been feeling some holy discontent, which we interpret as a prod from God to take a risk. We serve God through our jobs. Amy teaches reading at a public school among mostly at-risk kids. I'm a professor and pastor to pastors at a seminary. For both of us, work is not merely a career through which to earn a paycheck, but a mission through which to build God's kingdom. But we have become quite comfortable in our work. And, by now, we know that too much comfortable convenience can lead to the spiritual slump. In other words, it's time for a drastic decision!

At the time of this writing, we are aggressively exploring the possibility of starting a camp for at-risk kids in Marion, Indiana, where we live. The camp will provide an annual weeklong environment where children are lovingly treated like royalty, daughters and sons of King Jesus. In order to launch this mission, we will need to give hundreds of hours annually to recruit, train, and empower a large team of volunteers and to raise tens of thousands of dollars.

Some people close to us think we're crazy for adding this mammoth ministry to our rather full plates. Maybe we are. But we are also quite confident God is calling us out on a limb so that we, along with impoverished kids in our county, might experience his presence and power in profound ways.

Decision Time

God will nudge us toward decisions that have the potential to get us out of the slump and back on a streak.

Maybe it's time for you to get back to the basics with small, consistent decisions that cultivate your intimacy with God. Maybe God is calling you to make a drastic, borderline crazy decision that requires a risk of time, energy, money, reputation, or your life. Any decision, basic or drastic, that results from your yes to God is a sure way out of the spiritual slump.

In researching the baseball slump and how to get out of it, I observed a common tip: keep practicing! Spend more, not less, time in the batting practice cage. Repeating the swing will help you find your swing. Hitting is all about repetition, a mind-memory thing. We find ourselves in a spiritual slump when we repeat decisions of disobedience. The way out of a slump, then, is to decide on obedience to God repeatedly. A habit of obedience to God cultivates the spiritual muscle memory necessary for fulfilling and fruitful Christian living.

A repeated decision for David was to worship God no matter what was going on around him or in him. The Psalms bear this out. David worshiped no matter what! When he succeeded, he worshiped. When he failed, he worshiped. When he was disappointed with God, he worshiped. When he was on a spiritual streak, he worshiped. When he was in a slump, he worshiped. David worshiped his way out of the slumps that every disciple will inevitably encounter. That basic decision was life-giving.

Your turn. What two or three basic or drastic life-altaring decisions will you make in response to God's divine disruption? What "I won't" and "I will" decisions do you need to make now? Consider prayerfully drawing up your decision charter, your own version of Psalm 101.

A slumping baseball player's decision charter might include: "I will watch video of my swing after every game. I will meet with my hitting coach weekly. I will hit one hundred balls at practice daily. I will change my stance, step, and swing to get out of the slump." If a ball player is willing to make the basic and drastic decisions necessary to hit a red-threaded ball, how much more should we disciples be willing to do whatever it takes to live with faithful and joyful obedience to God?

Reflection

- What decisions have you made over the years to improve in your work, relationships, or hobbies? What sacrifices of time, energy, and/or money were necessary?

- Describe someone (a Bible character, friend, coworker, teammate, classmate, or family member) who made basic and/or drastic life-altaring decisions that God used to make that person more spiritually alive?

- What two to three basic decisions can you make in response to God's grace that might help you overcome the spiritual slump?
- Has God been nudging you out of your comfort zone to make a drastic decision that requires risk and sacrifice? What is the drastic life-altaring decision that God might use to initiate your movement from slump to streak?

Prayer

Lord, we want to partner with you in our growth as disciples of Christ. Guide us in making the decisions necessary to love you more and serve you better. Whatever you lay on our hearts, we will do with your help. May the decisions we make align with your "good, pleasing and perfect will" (Rom. 12:2b) for our lives. Amen.

CONCLUSION

David is the poster player for what it looks like to go from streak to slump to streak again. He experienced *degeneration* into boredom, adultery, and murder (see 2 Samuel 11). When he hit rock bottom, he was lifted up by the gracious *disruption* of the God who "sent Nathan to David" (2 Sam. 12:1a). After encountering the grace of God, David wrote Psalm 51, a prayer of *detestation* regarding his sin. Detesting our slump is not enough. In Psalm 32, David described the necessity of *disclosure*, noting how concealment kills, but confession heals. Then, David responded to God's grace with a series of *decisions*, basic and drastic, to partner with God in overcoming the slump (see Psalm 101).

I suppose the continuation of my story, that began in the first pages of this book, is in order. My journey, though unique, has a lot in common with David's story and maybe your story too.

Degeneration: I didn't come close to adultery or murder, but found myself in a slump, a spiritual midlife crisis, in my early forties. I'm not sure of the culprit, but I think it had something to do with my change of vocation from local church pastor to seminary professor. The truth is: I missed pastoral ministry. I longed for those days when I was with people who crossed the line of faith in Christ or stepped into the waters of baptism. It took me several years to figure out how to wear my professorial robe as a pastor to my students, most of whom are also pastors. Change of ministry vocation, change of location, change of friends, and simply hitting my fourth decade of life, I think, were contributing factors to my spiritual slump. I became stale and stuck, not wanting to engage in prayer, Scripture, or fellowship. Acedia hit me like a ton of bricks.

Disruption: In the same way that "the LORD sent Nathan to David" (2 Sam. 12:1a), the Lord sent people to me. He especially used my wife, Amy, to graciously disrupt my degeneration. She embodies a steady, humble, and deep faith in Christ. Her commitment to joyfully spend time in God's Word and prayer is infectious. She inspires me. Simply living with her, observing her ever-deepening intimacy with Christ, is a grace from God. Plus, she is not afraid to lovingly, graciously confront me like Nathan did for David. I found the grace of God in the face of my wife. God also used sermons, songs, friends, situations, books, and works of art to graciously disrupt my degeneration.

Detestation: Not having time and space for quiet reflection perpetuates the slump. We keep running and doing and going and scrolling and talking and tasking and texting. I finally stepped off of the hamster wheel. When I did, moments of silence and solitude allowed me to face the slump head-on. And I detested it, which was good. I have been in the habit of taking an annual three- to four-day retreat at a monastery. In fact, I lead a retreat for my students every year. Have you ever led a retreat for others while you were in a spiritual slump? Let me tell you, it's not easy. But those moments of silence and solitude that allowed space for deep reflection were theological therapy for my soul. I intensely detested my slump while simultaneously feeling the intense love of God for me. God's love for me made me detest my slump even more. I didn't detest myself because I love sin, but detested my sin because I love God. The difference is substantial.

Disclosure: Shortly after one of those monastic retreats, I did something risky but necessary. I suppose hanging out with monks for a few days had a weird effect on me. Anyway, I felt nudged by God to come clean and confess my slump to others. I needed a hitting coach, and I knew it. If I was going to overcome the spiritual slump, I wasn't going to do it alone. So, every month for six months, I disclosed my slump to a counselor and to a spiritual director. I also met monthly with a friend for breakfast. All of them asked me questions that helped me analyze the slump and employ practices to get back on a spiritual hitting streak. Was it hard to swallow my pride and let others help me? Yes! Did it require a sacrifice of time and money? Yes! Was it well worth the humility and sacrifice? Yes and yes!

Decision: When it comes to overcoming the spiritual slump, I've developed at least two primary convictions. First, God, by his grace, does the heavy lifting, the lion's share of the work. Second, I have a role to play in partnering with God to get back on a streak. God's grace is free, but I have to put myself in position to access it. So, I've made some basic decisions that positioned me well for grace. I take a prayer walk with Amy every morning. I'm reading through the Bible, a chapter every day. I pray one-on-one with each of my three teenage kids weekly. And I run on the treadmill four times each week. I've learned the hard way that there is an intricate connection between physical exercise and spiritual well-being.

There have been drastic decisions too, saying yes to God when there was a lot at stake. I said yes to serve as a mentor for Isaiah, an at-risk kid, and have been doing this almost weekly for the past eight years. I have said yes to preaching at camps, colleges, and churches when I felt slumpy. I said yes to serve as interim lead pastor of a local church when I wasn't sure how I would find the time. I'm not boasting about my capacity to say yes to God. To be transparent, I have said no to missional opportunities from God more often than I want to admit, usually because I was stuck in a self-absorbed slump. But on those few occasions when I accessed the grace to say yes to God, I felt lifted from the quagmire by his strong but tender hands.

I am living proof that God has the power to help disciples overcome their spiritual slump. As far as I can tell, many Christians are either heading into, stuck in, or coming out of the spiritual slump. The good news, that I hope comes through loud and clear in these pages, is that going through the slump can actually make us better ball players on the discipleship field than we've ever been. Plus, going through the slump enables us to help others who feel stuck in acedia. Perhaps this is why Jesus said, "first take the plank out of your own eye, and then you will see clearly to remove the speck from your brother's eye" (Matt. 7:5). In other words, our victory in certain areas gives us something of value to offer to those still engaged in the battle. I hope this book not only helps disciples, but assists those of you who disciple disciples.

Back to David. One of my favorite psalms of David is 103. I cry just about every time I read it. Bible scholars assert that David was quite old when he wrote this prayer.

Charles Spurgeon noted about this psalm of David: "we should attribute it to his later years when he had a higher sense of the preciousness of pardon, because a keener sense of sin, than in his younger days. This Psalm is as the apple tree among the trees of the wood, and its golden fruit has a flavour such as no fruit ever bears unless it has been ripened in the full sunshine of mercy."[6] David wrote this psalm after journeying from degeneration to disruption to detestation to disclosure to decision. Picture an old, wise man reflecting back on the ups and downs, the streaks and slumps, of his amazing life. What David professed in Psalm 103 became water in the spiritual aridity of my slump:

> Praise the LORD, my soul;
>> all my inmost being, praise his holy name.
> Praise the LORD, my soul,
>> and forget not all his benefits—
> who forgives all your sins
>> and heals all your diseases,
> who redeems your life from the pit
>> and crowns you with love and compassion,
> who satisfies your desires with good things
>> so that your youth is renewed like the eagle's.
>
> The LORD works righteousness
>> and justice for all the oppressed.

He made known his ways to Moses,
>> his deeds to the people of Israel:

The LORD is compassionate and gracious,
>> slow to anger, abounding in love.

He will not always accuse,
>> nor will he harbor his anger forever;

he does not treat us as our sins deserve
>> or repay us according to our iniquities.

For as high as the heavens are above the earth,
>> so great is his love for those who fear him;

as far as the east is from the west,
>> so far has he removed our transgressions from us.

As a father has compassion on his children,
>> so the LORD has compassion on those who
>> fear him;

for he knows how we are formed,
>> he remembers that we are dust.

The life of mortals is like grass,
>> they flourish like a flower of the field;

the wind blows over it and it is gone,
>> and its place remembers it no more.

But from everlasting to everlasting
>> the LORD's love is with those who fear him,
>> and his righteousness with their children's
>> children—

with those who keep his covenant
> and remember to obey his precepts.

The LORD has established his throne in heaven,
> and his kingdom rules over all.

Praise the LORD, you his angels,
> you mighty ones who do his bidding,
> who obey his word.

Praise the LORD, all his heavenly hosts,
> you his servants who do his will.

Praise the LORD, all his works
> everywhere in his dominion.

Praise the LORD, my soul.

The slump does not have to be your legacy. Slumps can happen to the best of players and disciples. In 1971, Luis Aparicio went 0 for 44. That's a gruesome slump. But he was still inducted into the Baseball Hall of Fame. The slump was not his legacy.

David had a bad year, too, spiritually speaking. He had a horrific slump, but still made it into the Hall of Fame or, better, the Hall of Faith in Hebrews 11. In that chapter, the author of Hebrews lists the heroes of the biblical story, including Noah, Abraham, Joseph, and Moses, to name a few. Then we see it in Hebrews 11:32—"David" is listed! Despite his wrinkles and flaws, David is a hero of the faith, "a man after [God's] own heart" (1 Sam. 13:14). The slump was not his legacy. Grace was.

The slump is not your legacy. You can take a thousand steps away from God, but it only takes one to come back.

If you're a child of the '80s like me, you know of Journey. And, if you're a true child of the '80s, you played the air guitar to Journey's *Don't Stop Believin'*. If you did, you should probably find an '80s music recovery group. Let me know if you find one, so I can go with you.

The ultimate message I believe God wants me to leave with you is, to borrow from Journey: don't stop believin'. Don't stop believin' that God can take away your bent toward sin. Don't stop believin' that God has undone the slump of the first Adam through the streak of the second Adam (Christ). Don't stop believin' that the coming of Christ reversed the curse of the fall so that we don't have to live with the consequences anymore. Don't stop believin' that the slump is not your identity or legacy. Don't stop believin' that God loves you with an everlasting, unconditional, and sanctifying love. Don't stop believin' that the God who created the world, parted the sea, and raised the dead can help you to overcome your spiritual slump!

Reflection

- Describe where you are or have been in the journey toward overcoming the spiritual slump.
- What do you think caused your *degeneration* into the slump?
- How has God's grace initiated a *disruption* of your degeneration?
- What was it like to go through a period of *detestation*, not hating yourself because you love sin but hating your sin because you love God?
- Have you found a hitting coach yet to whom you can *disclose* your slump and receive gracious guidance to get on a streak?
- What basic or drastic *decisions* have you made in response to God's disrupting grace?

Prayer

Lord, thank you for including the life of David in the biblical story. We resonate with his potential for both the streak and the slump. Thank you for showing us that, no matter how far we have fallen, we are never beyond the grip of your grace. Lord, enable us to track with David's journey of overcoming the slump so that our lives, in time, also reflect the legacy of your love. Amen.

APPENDIX
THE TRUE STORY OF A
MODERN-DAY DAVID

The Slump

My name is Jeff. Lenny asked me to share my story. So, here goes.

After being a youth and associate pastor for nearly eight years, my identity was entirely wrapped up in the image of a pastor. Serve the down-trodden, help the broken-hearted, love the un-loveable. That was me. But without a heart properly submitted to God and, therefore, without a properly checked ego, I truly thought *I* was *the* consummate pastor. I no longer credited God with successes, spiritual or otherwise. I stopped relying on him to fuel me through prayer, meditation, and devotion. I began thinking I really could be *all* things to all people. With that as my frame of mind and perceiving that I really deserved much more out of life than I was currently getting, I got selfish.

So along came a young woman who affirmed me and increased my self-esteem, making me feel better about myself than I had for months. Without the Holy Spirit fueling my identity and mission, I ate it up. She was a breath of fresh air, an angel really, but one with broken wings. She helped me feel better about myself, and I wanted to help her too.

We initially met for coffee once every couple of months, a not-so-unusual occurrence for a pastor. Public place, plenty of witnesses, lots of accountability; it was fine. But then she needed a place to stay and, wouldn't you know, my wife and I had an unused guest room in our house. We took her in. I'd like to think that it was all still innocent at this point, but there is a piece of me that knows I had been scoping out my Bathsheba from the moment I met her. Without the power of a king like David, it just took a little longer for me to cross the line.

As with every secret affair, "Whatever is hidden is meant to be disclosed, and whatever is concealed is meant to be brought out into the open" (Mark 4:22). After an emotional affair that lasted about six weeks and a physical one that took up about three of those weeks, I came clean late one night. My wife, unwittingly playing the part of Nathan, asked the right questions, and my heart could not resist the conviction it felt. I spilled all the beans.

That very night I was out of the house, out of a ministry, and out of ego. Within a week I had lost my credentials, my enrollment in seminary, and any hope that I could get out of this mess. Fast-forward to night of exile number six. I found myself on my (gay, divorced, sex offender) dad's sofa—the last place I ever thought I'd be, and with the one man I had sworn to never be like. With the house quiet and the voices in my head screaming, I finally broke. Every last ounce of will and ego within me admitted that I was a mess, wholly unable to be holy, and so far down the rabbit hole that I deserved nothing less than to be given over to the darkness within. I cried! Constantly! I begged God for any sort of grace or redemption or help, but why would he give it to one so despicable? My life as I knew it was over. I thought.

The Grace

In that moment, my phone rang. I saw my pastor's number. I served as his assistant pastor. He was my boss. Correction: *former* boss. The man who had invested in me, believed in me, and elevated me. Him. The one I had let down and, in effect, trampled on.

"Hello?"

"Jeff, I just felt like I needed to call you. I was pretty hard on you last time we talked. But this time, I want to make sure you know I love you. And I'm not going to ditch you. That's all."

"Um, OK. Thanks?"

"That's not good enough. Tell me you're not going to ditch me too. Then we can hang up."

I stuttered, "I, um, I'm not going to ditch you, either."

He finished with, "Good enough. Good night, Jeff. It's going to be a long, hard road, but I'm here with you. I won't ditch you. Goodbye."

Click. That was it. Thirty seconds, tops. But in that moment, I knew that there was hope and light, life and redemption, available to me. Someone wasn't going to ditch me, which led me to conclude: neither would God. I broke down and wept more intensely than ever. This time, however, the tears were my soul submitting to him, come what may.

The Streak

It has been nine years since my affair, the fallout, and the redemption. Full restoration is happening. If Job is any proof, God can lead us to even better places than we experienced before the spiritual slump. My life is submitted to God now. He is first. With a heart rightfully submitted to him and the ego in check, humility will help me thrive.

Once my relationship with God was restored, he started to guide my reconciliation with others. He has miraculously restored my marriage. My wife and I seek to love each other without reserve. It is a more beautiful and fulfilling marriage than either of us ever imagined possible, especially after my major debacle! God has restored my relationship with my step-daughter, as she saw me work so hard to take care of her mother and be a good husband. And God has restored my relationship with my son so that he no longer mentions "that time when you weren't here for a long time." He is thrilled about the new memories we're creating together as a family.

Everything else beyond the restoration of my marriage and family is icing on the cake. But that icing is rich and tasty! The local church I disappointed managed the grace to minister to my wife and me so beautifully. They made a request to denominational leaders that I be reinstated as a pastor after going through a restoration process. I was allowed to return to seminary and have finally graduated! The denomination has received, restored, and ordained me. After a long desert period in various occupations, I am now a church planter and part-time Bible teacher at a high school.

Under the lordship of Christ, my life is vibrant, blossoming, and full of life-affirming grace. All of this only happened because I finally surrendered control of my life to the God of all grace. It is a paradox of faith that submission to God brings freedom in life, but it is absolutely true. Even after the slumps, losses, and defeats in my life, I can proudly say that God has enabled me to be a far better and more fulfilled man than I ever imagined I could be. David's dying words echo through the generations to me today: "So be strong, act like a man, and observe what the LORD your God requires: Walk in obedience to him, and keep his decrees and commands, his laws and regulations, as written in the Law of Moses. Do this so that you may prosper in all you do and wherever you go" (1 Kings 2:2b–3).

Sincerely grateful to God,
Jeff

NOTES

1. Francis Thompson, "The Hound of Heaven," *The Hound of Heaven* (New York: Dodd, Mead and Company, 1926). Public domain.

2. Oswald Chambers, *My Utmost for His Highest*, "The Concentration of Personal Sin," (Uhrichsville, OH: Barbour and Company, 1935), 185.

3. See https://housechurch.org/miscellaneous/wesley_band -societies.html.

4. Charles Wesley, "A Prayer for Children," in *Hymns for Children*, #473, 1763. See http://www.ccel.org/ccel/wesley /hymn/jwg04/jwg0473.html.

5. See https://www.espn.com/mlb/story/_/id/7911483/being -slump-feeling-unique-baseball.

6. See https://www.christianity.com/bible/commentary.php?com =spur&b=19&c=103.